£4-99

D1096111

THE HUNGRY MONK
AT WORK

A NEW BOOK OF SECRETS
from
CLAIRE BURGESS and THAI LA ROCHE
written by
NIGEL and SUE MACKENZIE
with drawings by Graham Jeffery

HUNGRY MONK PUBLICATIONS
Jevington, Near Polegate
Sussex BN26 5QF

Telephone 0323 483989 or 482178

Also in the same series:-

The Secrets of the Hungry Monk
The Deeper Secrets of the Hungry Monk
The Hungry Monk at Home
The Secret Sauce Book
Cooking with the Hungry Monk

First published November 1991

THIS BOOK IS DEDICATED TO
IAN DOWDING, THE FIRST HEAD CHEF OF
THE HUNGRY MONK

CONTENTS

STARTERS

MAIN COURSES

Fish
Fillets of Salmon with Yellow Pepper and Prawn Sauce............................ 43
Scallops and Brill with Two Sauces - Choron and Beurre Blanc............ 44
Sole in Lettuce with Scallop Mousseline... 46
Red Mullet with Sun-Dried Tomatoes.. 48
Salmon and Asparagus in Filo with Hollandaise....................................... 49
Monkfish with Mushroom and Vermouth Sauce... 50

Beef
Medallions of Fillet Steak with Wild Mushroom Sauce............................ 51
Feuillete of Beef with Oysters... 52
Roast Sirloin with Garlic, Shallots and Red Wine.................................... 54

Lamb
Fillet of Lamb in Filo with Pesto and Rosemary Sauce............................ 56
Rack of Lamb with Flageolet Beans and Garlic... 58

Pork
Tenderloin of Pork in Pastry with Apricot Stuffing................................... 61
Cassoulet of Pork and Duck.. 63

Game
Roast Grouse with Port and Redcurrant Sauce............................ 65
Saddle of Rabbit with Prunes and Dijon Mustard Sauce...................... 66
Roast Pheasant with Chestnut and Sherry Sauce............................ 68
Venison with Cassis and Shallots... 70

Poultry
Marinated Guinea Fowl with Yoghurt and Cumin................................ 71
Breast of Duck with Passion Fruit and Marsala Sauce........................ 72
Breast of Chicken with Watercress Sauce.. 74

Liver
Calves Liver with Raspberry Vinegar and Cream Sauce...................... 76

Vegetarian
Vegetarian Cous-Cous... 77
Marinated Kebab with Two Sorts of Rice and Apricots...................... 78
Spinach and Gruyere Souffle with Sweet Pepper Sauce...................... 80

VEGETABLES

PUDDINGS

MISCELLANEOUS

TOMATO AND BASIL SOUP

This soup can be served hot or chilled

To serve 4

> 2 lb/l kilo English Tomatoes
> 1 medium onion
> 1 medium potato
> 2 oz/50 grms unsalted butter
> 1 pt/600 ml vegetable or chicken stock
> 1/4 pt/150 ml medium white wine
> 1/4 pt/150 ml double cream
> a clove of garlic
> 8 sprigs of fresh basil
> salt and freshly ground black pepper
> a little sour cream
> chopped parsley

Preparation

Roughly chop the tomatoes and the potato. Peel and finely chop the onion and garlic. Chop 2 sprigs of the basil and set aside.

Method

Take a large saucepan and melt the butter to cook the onion and garlic until soft but not coloured. Then simply tip in all the remaining ingredients except for the 2 sprigs of chopped basil and the cream. Bring briefly to the boil before simmering for 30 - 35 minutes. Transfer the soup to a liquidiser and blend to a smooth consistency before passing through a sieve to remove the skin and pips. Don't use too fine a sieve or it will take all day! Pour the soup in to a clean saucepan and reheat gently stirring in the cream and chopped basil. Check the seasoning.

Serve with a swirl of sour cream and chopped parsley. If you are feeling gutsy and can lay your hands on a thin baguette - chop it in to slices, brush them with garlic butter and bake in a hot oven for 6 - 8 minutes before serving on top of the soup.

CURRIED SEAFOOD SOUP WITH FRESH CORIANDER YOGHURT

To serve 6

6 oz/150 grms crabmeat - fresh or frozen
1 lb/450 grms mixed seafood such as salmon,
  squid, mussels, prawns, haddock
4 shallots
2 oz/50 grms butter
1/2 pt/300 ml double cream
1/4 pt/150 ml dry white wine
2 oz/50 grms long grain rice
2 heaped teaspoonfuls of curry paste
1 teaspoonful of ground cumin
1 teaspoonful of ground coriander
1 teaspoonful of ground caraway
salt and freshly ground black pepper

The Stock

1 lb/450 grms fish bones and skins
  (ask your fishmonger for these)
2 pts/1.2 litres water
1/2 pt/300 ml dry white wine
2 sticks of celery
5 carrots
half a lemon
2 star annis
a bouquet garni
1 teaspoon of black peppercorns

Preparation
To make the fish stock - take a large heavy based pan and toss in the fish
trimmings, celery, carrots, lemon, star annis, bouquet garni and black
peppercorns. Cover with the water and wine, bring sharply to the boil and
simmer at a good pace for 20 to 30 minutes to reduce to 2 pts/1.2 litres.
Strain and reserve the stock.
Peel and finely chop the shallots. Cut the salmon and haddock in to 1/2 in.
cubes.

Method

Take a large saucepan and melt the butter. Cook the shallots with the
cumin, caraway, coriander and curry paste until soft. Tip in the rice,
crabmeat, fish stock, wine, salt and black pepper. Bring to the boil.
Simmer for 25 - 30 minutes before transferring to a liquidiser. Blend until
smooth. Pour in to a clean saucepan and heat through. At this stage we
are ready to tip in the fish and seafood but it is important to be as gentle as
possible to stop it breaking up. Continue to cook for 5 - 10 minutes until all
the fish is cooked. Very gently fold in the cream. Check the seasoning
and serve with a dollop of Coriander Yoghurt.

To make Coriander Yoghurt

Take a 1/2 pt/300 ml tub of Greek yoghurt and stir in 3 tablespoonfuls of
freshly chopped coriander leaves.

WATERCRESS SOUP

This soup can be served hot or chilled

To serve 4

> 4 bunches of watercress
> 1 medium onion
> 1 medium potato
> 2 oz/50 grms butter
> 1/2 pt/300 ml double cream
> 1 pt/600 ml chicken or vegetable stock
> 1/4 pt/150 ml dry white wine
> salt and freshly ground black pepper

Preparation

Peel and roughly chop the onion and potato. Trim the ends of the watercress stalks and discard. The idea now is to cut the leaves from the bunches and finely chop them ready to be added at the last minute to the soup. The remaining stalks should be roughly chopped.

Method

Take a large saucepan and melt the butter. Cook the onion until soft before adding the stock, wine, potato, watercress stalks, salt and pepper. Bring to the boil and allow to simmer for 25 - 30 minutes. Remove from the heat and transfer to a liquidiser. Blend to a smooth consistency and pass through a medium sieve. Pour the soup in to a clean saucepan, add the leaves and gently heat through for 5 minutes before stirring in the cream. Check the seasoning.

One word of caution:- the reason that we have left adding the leaves until the last minute is to ensure that the soup has a wonderful fresh green colour. Once it is heated through serve it immediately. If you leave it bubbling away you will lose colour and taste.

ASPARAGUS AND SMOKED SALMON TART

To serve 6   8 oz/225 grms rich shortcrust pastry

The Filling   6 oz/150 grms sliced smoked salmon
                     6 spears of fresh asparagus
                     1 egg
                     1 egg yolk
                     1/4 pt/150 ml double cream
                     1/4 pt/150 ml milk
                     a few sprigs of fresh dill
                     salt and freshly ground black pepper

Equipment - 6 x 4 in. diameter, 1 1/4 in. deep loose-bottomed tart
     tins
     greaseproof paper
     baking beans

Preparation
Preheat the oven to No.6/400 degrees.
We need to bake the six pastry cases 'blind'
Trim off one inch from the base of the asparagus sticks.   Poach them taking
care to keep the tips out of the water.   This is ideally done in an asparagus
poacher.   Drain the asparagus before cutting 3 in. of the tip to reserve for
decoration and roughly chopping the remainder.   Chop the dill. Finely chop
the smoked salmon.
Reduce the heat in the oven to No.5/375 degrees.

Method
Start by placing the eggs in a bowl.   Add the milk and cream and whisk
well.   Then tip in the smoked salmon, dill, salt and black pepper.   Place the
chopped asparagus in equal parts in the bottom of the pastry cases and
pour over the egg and salmon mixture.   Decorate with the 3 in. asparagus
spears and bake in the oven on a baking tray for 20 to 30 minutes or until
set and golden topped.

This is delicious served with watercress or if you are feeling energetic make a **Sweet Pepper Sauce** by cooking 3 de-seeded, finely chopped peppers in a covered saucepan with a splash of white wine vinegar, a glass of dry sherry, a little water, salt and freshly ground black pepper. Cook until soft before sieving to a smooth puree to serve warm.

Variation for Vegetarians
Instead of the smoked salmon crumble in 6 oz/175 grms goat's cheese.

Rich Short Crust Pastry
We have found this pastry ideal for quiches and tarts as it moulds easily in to the flan tin, bakes really crisply and in using more than half fat to flour we prevent shrinkage when baking blind.

Rich Short Crust Pastry
> 8 oz/225 grms plain flour
> 5 oz/150 grms unsalted butter
> 1 egg
> cold water
> a pinch of salt

Method
Sieve the flour with the salt in to a bowl. Cut the butter in to pieces and rub in to the flour until the consistency of fine breadcrumbs has been achieved. Make a well in the centre of the flour and first crack the egg in to this followed by as much water as half of the eggshell holds. Work with the fingertips to a smooth dough.

To Bake Blind
Preheat the oven to No.6/400 degrees.
Roll out the pastry onto a floured board and line the flan tins. Hold the pastry in place during cooking by lining with greaseproof paper and a layer of baking beans. Place on a baking tray and cook in the preheated oven until the visible edges of the pastry are just turning gold. Remove the paper and beans and continue to cook until the base is just crisp.

THAI PRAWNS

Prawns and Vegetables served hot in a spicy liquor.

To serve 4 - 6

6 king prawns - for decoration
12 oz/300 grms cooked and peeled prawns
4 spring onions
1 green, red and yellow pepper
2 sticks of celery
a small tin of water chestnuts

The Marinade

2 tablespoonfuls of vegetable oil
1/4 pt/150 ml dry white wine
1 oz/25 grms fresh root ginger
a clove of garlic
1 heaped teaspoonful of five spices
2 tablespoonfuls of light soy sauce
1 tablespoonful of Dijon mustard
2 tablespoonfuls of clear honey
2 tablespoonfuls of white wine vinegar
3 shakes of tabasco
freshly ground black pepper

Preparation

If the prawns you have are frozen - thaw them and drain. Finely slice in to strips the peppers, onions, celery, water chestnuts. Peel and grate the root ginger. Peel and finely chop the garlic.
These ingredients except the prawns will be steeped in the following marinade for at least 2 hours.

To make the marinade

Take a decent-sized bowl and put in the bottom all the marinade ingredients except for the white wine and oil. These should be poured in oil first then the wine whilst whisking continuously to form a smooth emulsion not unlike french dressing. Check the seasoning.

Method
Take a heavy based saute pan. Spoon in the marinade mixture and bring sharply to the boil. Simmer for a few moments before tipping in the prawns to heat them through. Add a little more white wine if you feel things are looking a bit dry. All that remains is to slice the king prawns down the middle and flash them under the grill before decorating the dish.

Serve with either a little salad or a blini or a on rice or, if you are bursting with confidence, a basket made of strips of deep fried potato!!

A quick approach
One of our head chefs is from Thailand and he has a very different and much quicker approach to preparing this dish. He dispenses with the marinade and prefers to use a wok over a high flame.
First he tips in the oil, followed by the garlic and ginger; cooks for a moment before tipping in all the remaining ingredients except for the vegetables and prawns. He cooks for a minute or two longer, stirring all the time, adds in the prepared vegetables, followed after a few more minutes by the peeled prawns. Finally he checks the seasoning and serves decorated with the king prawns as above.

A SALAD OF KIPPER FILLETS

A much neglected item - the kipper fillet is light, moist and jolly tasty when served with poached green beans and apples.

To serve 4	8 oz/225 grms kipper fillets
	10 black peppercorns
	2 bay leaves
	3 slices of lemon
	a glass of dry white wine
	water
	8 oz/225 grms french beans
	2 eating apples
	1 red onion
	8 cherry tomatoes
	a little vegetable oil
The Dressing	1 egg yolk
	2 dessertspoonfuls of white wine vinegar
	1 dessertspoonful of Dijon mustard
	3 tablespoonfuls of horseradish sauce
	a small glass of dry white wine
	4 tablespoonfuls of double cream
	1/4 pt/150 ml olive oil
	a little caster sugar
	chopped chives
	the juice of half a lemon
	salt and freshly ground black pepper

Preparation

Place the kipper fillets in a covered pan just submerged in the wine and water with the peppercorns, bay leaves and lemon slices. Poach for 8 - 10 minutes. Drain, cool and flake the fish from the skin.

Top and tail the beans. Poach lightly, drain and refresh under cold running water until cold. Drain again. Peel, core and slice the apples and prevent them from going brown by squeezing over a little lemon juice. Peel and finely slice the onion. Cut the tomatoes in half.

Method
To make the dressing, start by making an emulsion by placing the egg yolk, mustard and vinegar in a bowl and whisking on the oil. Next stir in the cream, horseradish and enough white wine to produce a thick, creamy dressing. Add the chives and lemon juice. Season with salt and black pepper. Taste and then add enough caster sugar to produce an overall flavour which is balanced to ensure that there is not too strong a taste of vinegar.

Assembly
We have discovered that this dish will always look better if you can assemble it just before serving. Start by bringing together the beans, apples, onions and tomatoes. Pour on the dressing and stir gently. Finally introduce the kipper fillets in to the salad as gently as possible in order to prevent the fish from breaking up.

Serve with a little green salad or as an open sandwich on dark rye bread.

BABY SQUID STUFFED WITH SPICED RICE

To serve 4	8 Baby Squid
The Stuffing	3 oz/75 grms basmati rice
	1/2 pt/300 ml chicken stock
	1/4 pt/150 ml dry white wine
	half a red pepper
	2 tomatoes
	1 dessertspoonful of tomato puree
	1 small onion
	2 oz/50 grms unsalted butter
	a clove of garlic
	a pinch of powdered cumin
	1 tablespoonful of chopped chives
	a bay leaf
	salt, freshly ground black pepper and tabasco
	greaseproof paper

Preparation

In all probability your baby squid will come ready prepared. However should you be buying them fresh from the market it is necessary to grasp the head and reach inside to pull out and discard the whitish transparent guts. Then cut off and save the tentacles, discarding the head.

Preheat the oven to No.5/375 degrees.

Peel the tomatoes by slitting across the tops and immersing in boiling water for around one minute. De-seed them and roughly chop.

Next peel and chop the garlic and onion. De-seed and chop the red pepper. Wash the rice under cold water and drain.

Cut a circle of greaseproof paper to fit the saucepan that you will use to make the stuffing.

Method

The stuffing is made in a heavy based pan. Start by melting the butter and cooking the garlic, onion and red pepper for around 2 minutes. Tip in the rice and saute for another 2 minutes, stirring from time to time. Now add the tomatoes, tomato puree and stock, followed by the cumin, bay leaf, salt and black pepper. Maintain over a medium heat for about 15 minutes to allow the mixture to bubble away, stirring occasionally, until there is a thin covering of liquor over the surface of the rice. Remove the pan from the heat and cover the surface of the stuffing with the circle of greaseproof paper. Put on the lid and return to a very low flame for another 5 minutes.

All that remains is to allow the mixture to cool sufficiently to handle. Add a few shakes of tabasco, check the seasoning and stuff the rice in to the 8 raw squid. Finally arrange the stuffed squid in a baking dish, pour around the white wine. Cover with foil and cook in the oven for 15 minutes.

Serve with a-

Fresh Tomato Provencale Sauce

1 lb/450 grms peeled tomatoes - fresh or tinned
1 Spanish onion
1 glass of dry white wine
2 fl oz/60 ml olive oil
2 cloves of garlic
a large pinch of Herbes de Provence
a little sugar
salt and freshly ground black pepper

Method

Peel and slice the onion. Roughly chop the tomatoes. Crush the garlic with a little salt. Saute the onions and garlic in the oil until transparent. Toss in the herbs followed by the wine and bring briefly to the boil. Finally add the tomatoes and season with sugar, salt and black pepper. Simmer for 15 minutes.

STUFFED NEW ZEALAND GREEN LIPPED MUSSELS

These mussels taste as good as they look being twice the size of any other mussel and set in a beautiful opalescant green shell (available from good supermarkets and fishmongers)

To serve 4

16 New Zealand green-lipped mussels in half shells

The Stuffing	The Topping
10 oz/250 grms cream cheese	4 oz/100 grms breadcrumbs
5 oz/125 grms kassler or ham	2 oz/50 grms grated parmesan
1 shallot	2 sprigs of parsley
1 teaspoonful of curry paste	
1 dessertspoonful of mango chutney	
a little vegetable oil	
2 sprigs of fresh coriander	
salt and freshly ground black pepper	

Preparation
Preheat the oven to No.7/425 degrees. The following ingredients need to be finely chopped:- parsley, coriander, kassler or ham and shallots which should be fried in a little oil until soft. Mix together the breadcrumbs, parmesan and parsley.

Method
The stuffing will be spread over the top of each mussel in its shell. This is made by combining the cream cheese with the chopped kassler (or ham), mango chutney, curry paste and cooked shallots. Using a dessert spoon as a mould scoop a spoonful of the mixture on to the top of each mussel and finish with a coating of the breadcrumb mixture.

Arrange the mussels in an ovenproof dish. Sprinkle with a little vegetable oil and bake in the preheated oven for 8 - 10 minutes until golden.

Serve with hot garlic bread and salad or more deliciously with **Vermouth Sauce** the recipe for which appears on page 50.

SMOKED SALMON STUFFED WITH SMOKED TROUT MOUSSE

To serve 4

4 slices of smoked salmon
1/2 lb/225 grms smoked trout fillets
2 1/2 leaves of gelatine
1/2 pt/300 ml double cream
the juice of 2 lemons
a pinch of nutmeg
a sprig of dill
salt and freshly ground black pepper

Preparation

Flake the smoked trout from the skin.   Soften the leaves of gelatine in cold water and drain.

Method

We commence by making the smoked trout mousse.   This is ideally done in a liquidiser or magimix.   Simply puree the smoked trout with salt, black pepper, nutmeg and dill.   Then heat the lemon juice and stir in the softened gelatine.   Restart the magimix and pour on the gelatine solution followed immediately by the cream.   Stop the machine and with a rubber spatula ensure that all the cream is fully integrated.   Transfer to a bowl to allow to set in the fridge for about 2 hours.

Assembly

Simply lay the slices of smoked salmon on a board, divide the mousse equally between the six slices and wrap each up in to a parcel.

Serve surrounded by **Green Mayonnaise** and decorated with mock (or real!) caviar and watercress.

Green Mayonaise

1/2 pt/300 ml vegetable oil
2 egg yolks
the juice of 2 lemons
l dessertspoonful of Dijon mustard
salt and freshly ground black pepper
a small bunch of watercress
a few young spinach leaves
a few sprigs of parsley
a sprig of tarragon

21

Preparation

Trim an inch off the watercress stalks. Remove the stalks from the spinach leaves. Bring a small amount of water to the boil and plunge in all the green ingredients to blanch them. Drain and squeeze dry in a tea towel. Puree in a liquidiser or pass through a medium sieve.

Method

To make the mayonnaise place the egg yolks in a mixing bowl and blend in the mustard together with a little salt and black pepper. It is necessary to alternately beat in small quantities of a thin stream of oil until the mixture becomes very thick and then thin it down with lemon juice. Continue this process, maintaining an even consistency until all the oil has been absorbed. Stir in the green puree and adjust the seasoning.

GREEN BEAN, WATER CHESTNUT AND CUCUMBER SALAD

To serve 4

12 oz/350 grms French green beans
4 oz/100 grms tinned water chestnuts
half a cucumber
1 tablespoonful of chopped chives

For the Dressing

1/2 pt/300ml olive oil
1 large clove of garlic
a small glass of white wine
1 egg yolk
3 tablespoonfuls of double cream or Greek yoghurt
1 dessertspoonful of mustard
4 dessertspoonfuls of white wine vinegar
1 teaspoonful of sugar
salt and freshly ground black pepper

assorted lettuce leaves

Preparation
Top and tail the beans and bring sharply to the boil in just enough salted water to cover before draining and refreshing under running cold water. Slice the cucumber lengthways in to half inch batons. Drain and slice the water chestnuts. Crush the garlic with a little salt.

Method
The secret of this dish is in the quality of the dressing. Place the egg yolk in a small pudding basin and whisk in the mustard, sugar, vinegar, crushed garlic, salt and black pepper. Next whisk in the oil in a thin stream followed by the yoghurt or cream (depending on how rich you like your dressing). Finally stir in enough white wine to achieve a well balanced flavour with the consistency of single cream. It only remains to toss in the chives. Allow to stand for 20 minutes for the flavours to fully develop. Just before serving combine the dressing with the french beans, water chestnuts and cucumber. To assemble the salad Arrange a selection of washed and dried lettuce leaves to form a base and then simply spoon on the green bean mixture. Serve with hot crusty french bread.

TOASTED GOATS CHEESE WITH SESAME SEEDS

Utterly simple to prepare - an ideal starter or light lunch for people on a diet!

To serve 6

Goat's cheese comes in many varieties from very soft and fresh to quite old and hard. This recipe requires something in the middle that is soft enough to allow it to be mixed with cream cheese. Look out for the pyramid or log shaped goat's cheese as this is generally ideal.

12 oz/350 grms goat's cheese
8 oz/225 grms Philadelphia cream cheese
6 oz/150 grms sesame seeds
a little sesame seed or olive oil
6 slices of bread

Preparation
Preheat the oven to gas mark 6/400 degrees. Sprinkle the sesame seeds on a baking tray and dribble the oil over them. Very lightly toast in the oven. Remove and allow to cool.
Next the toast - no mystery about this, simply make in the usual way before cutting in to six rounds with a crinkle edged cutter.
Should your goat's cheese have an ash or rind outer protection, trim it off and discard.

Method
This is another job that is ideal for a food processor as we need to blend together the two cheeses. Once blended divide the cheese in to six equal parts the shape of deep fish cakes with an overall diameter the same size as the round toast. Roll the cheeses in the sesame seeds. Position on the toast and cook on a baking tray in a gas mark 7/425 degrees for 6 - 8 minutes just before serving. Be careful only to cook them long enough to be just golden as overcooking will cause the cheese to break up.
Serve either with a simple salad or fresh tomato sauce or just watercress with french dressing.

SALAD OF GRILLED MIXED PEPPERS

To serve 4

2 large green peppers
2 large red peppers
1 large yellow pepper
black and green olives
a little vegetable oil

For the French Dressing

10 tablespoonfuls of olive oil
10 tablespoonfuls of vegetable oil
1 egg yolk
1 dessertspoonful of mustard
1 teaspoonful of sugar
2 dessertspoonfuls of white wine vinegar
a clove of garlic
a sprig of fresh basil
a sprig of fresh mint
salt and freshly ground black pepper

assorted lettuce leaves

Preparation

Stone and halve the olives. Crush the garlic with a little salt. Finely chop
the fresh basil and mint.
Make the French Dressing by whisking the ingredients together in the
following order:- first the mustard with the sugar, egg yolk, garlic, salt and
black pepper, followed by the vinegar and finally the olive oil which should
be poured in as a thin stream whisking all the time. Stir in the fresh
herbs.
Slice the peppers down the middle and scrape out all the seeds.
Preheat the grill to maximum.

Method

Brush the outside of the peppers with a little oil. Arrange them on a grill
pan and put under the flame for as long as it takes for the skins to blacken
(at this stage you should be able to peel off the burnt skin). Remove from
the flame and having de-skinned the peppers slice them in to thin batons
and mix together in the french dressing with the olives.
Allow to stand for a little while before serving on a bed of lettuce with hot
crusty bread or on grilled Ciabatta bread.

MUSHROOMS EN BRIOCHE

Mushrooms cooked in anchovy and garlic butter and presented in a hollowed out brioche.

To serve 4	**12 oz/300 grms field or cultivated flat mushrooms - not button or cup mushrooms**
	4 oz/100 grms cream cheese
	2 oz/50 grms butter
	3 anchovy fillets
	2 shallots
	a clove of garlic
	3 sprigs of fresh basil
	2 teaspoonfuls of Worcestershire sauce
	6 tablespoonfuls of double cream
	salt and freshly ground black pepper
The Brioche	**9 oz/225 grms strong plain flour**
	2 oz/50 grms butter
	2 eggs
	1/2 oz/12 grms fresh yeast
	3 tablespoonfuls of warm water
	1 teaspoonful of caster sugar
	a large pinch of salt
	1 egg
	half a cup of milk
Equipment	**4 Brioche tins**

Preparation

First we must make the brioche dough.   In a bowl crumble the yeast in to the warm water, stir in the sugar and 2 tablespoonfuls of the flour.   Cover and leave in a warm place for about 20 minutes until frothy.   Take a large warm bowl and tip in the rest of the flour and the salt.

Rub the butter in to this flour until the mixture resembles breadcrumbs. Whisk the eggs in to the bowl of frothy yeast batter and then tip this mixture in to the flour and butter. Work to a smooth dough and then knead until smooth and elastic. Place in a buttered polythene bag and leave in a warm place until doubled in size. Butter the brioche tins. Make an egg wash by beating the egg in to the milk. Wipe the mushrooms and trim the stalks. Puree the anchovies. Crush the garlic with a little salt. Finely chop the shallots and the basil.

Method
Once the brioche dough has doubled in size remove it from the polythene, knock it back and divide it in to four equal pieces. Cut off a chunk from each to form the tops. Roll the four pieces in to a round bun and also the four tops in to rounds. Transfer to the brioche tins and stick on the tops with egg wash. Cover the brioches with oiled cling film and leave in a warm place to prove for about 30 minutes until puffy. Preheat the oven to gas mark 7/425 degrees. Brush with egg wash and place on a baking tray in the oven to cook for 15 to 20 minutes until browned. Remove from the oven, tip out of their tins and allow to cool on a wire rack.
Now the filling. Heat the butter and fry the shallots, garlic, mushrooms and anchovies until soft. Remove from the heat and allow to cool before stirring in the cream cheese, cream, Worcestershire sauce and basil and seasoning with salt and black pepper.

Assembly
Carefully cut the tops off the brioches and place to one side. Then scoop out the centres with a spoon leaving the walls approximately half an inch thick. Now warm through the mushroom mixture and spoon generously in to the brioche cases. Replace the lids and bake on an ovenproof tray for 2 minutes. Serve with watercress.

FEUILLETE OF BRIE WITH CRANBERRIES

Brie cooked in puff pastry on a bright red sauce.

To serve 4
14 oz/400 grms just ripe Brie
13 oz/375 grms pack of frozen puff pastry
8 oz/225 grms frozen cranberries
4 oz/100 grms caster sugar
1 oz/25 grms unsalted butter
1/4 pt/150 ml orange juice
a small glass of port
1 egg
half a cup of milk

Preparation
Defrost the pastry. Trim the rind from the Brie and discard. Roughly chop the Brie and beat to a creamy consistency. Beat the egg in to the milk to make the egg wash.

Method
The idea with this dish is to line a cup or an individually sized pudding basin with the pastry. Do this by first rolling out the pastry on to a floured surface sufficiently large to allow you to cut out four circles or 9 in. diameter and four more of just 2 in. diameter.

Take the four large circles and in order to make it easier for them to fit in to the cup, cut a slit in each circle of about 1.5 in. in length from the outer edge towards the centre, sealing the slit with egg wash.

Next divide the cheese in to four equal parts and push gently in to the lined cups.

Now lay the small circle of pastry on the top of the cheese. Brush with egg wash and fold the pastry sides down on top to make a seal. It is vital that this seal should be watertight if you are to prevent the Brie pouring out during the cooking that is to come.

Turn out the uncooked Brie puddings on to a baking tray and allow to rest for half an hour in the fridge.

This is a good opportunity to put on the oven to gas mark 7/425 degrees and to make the Cranberry Sauce. This is simply done by placing the cranberries in a saucepan with the port, orange juice, caster sugar and boiling until the cranberries have popped open. Pass through a medium sieve in to a clean saucepan. Just before serving place over the heat and stir in the butter to give the sauce a shine.

Going back to the Brie puddings, these should be baked, having first cut an air hole in to their tops and brushed them with egg wash. Cook for 10 to 15 minutes until golden and serve on warmed plates surrounded by the Cranberry Sauce. (Do not pour the sauce over them as this will ruin the dish).

A WORD ABOUT WARM SALADS

Warm salads seem such a natural dish nowadays that it is hard to remember a time without them. They are immensely versatile, being quite simply a hot ingredient served in a warm dressing on a bed of lettuce leaves drawn from four or five different varieties (most supermarkets do a bag of mixed lettuce leaves).

We make our base from the following lettuces:- oak leaf, lollo rosso, frisee, radiccio, plus chicory and watercress, each brushed with a little walnut or hazlenut oil. The arrangement should be built up like an overblown garden rose with the largest leaves in a circle round the plate first and then the other leaves in descending size layered on top. In each case the hot mixture will be positioned in the centre of all this. We always finish by sprinkling something crisp on top such as croutons, toasted pine kernels and best of all crisp bacon and a fresh herb such as a few leaves of coriander, parsley, chives or basil.

It goes without saying that a warm salad can be served as a starter or a main course.

A WARM SALAD OF CHICKEN LIVERS

To serve 4	1 lb/450 grms chicken livers
	4 rashers of smoked streaky bacon

For the Dressing	1 dessertspoonful of vegetable oil
	2 dessertspoonfuls of white wine vinegar
	a small glass of madeira or dry sherry
	a small glass of white wine
	salt and freshly ground black pepper
	half a clove of garlic
	salt
	assorted lettuce leaves
	croutons

Preparation

Commence by trimming the sinews and any tubes from the livers. Crush the garlic with a little salt. Grill the bacon until crisp and roughly crumble.

Method

Prepare and arrange the salad - see page 31. Heat the oil and cook the garlic until it just turns golden. Toss in the livers and maintain over a high heat until blood starts to ooze. This is the moment to pour in the vinegar, madeira or sherry, wine, salt and black pepper. Reduce slightly. Spoon on to the waiting lettuce leaves and sprinkle with the bacon and croutons. Serve immediately!

A WARM SALAD OF CONFIT OF DUCK

As so many dishes made with duck use only the breast this is a welcome and delicious way of serving the legs - crisp and tender with a delicious dressing.

To serve 4

For the Confit	4 duck legs
	1 pt/600 ml duck fat or white Flora
	1 dessertspoonful of juniper berries
	3 bay leaves
	1 dessertspoonful of black peppercorns
	1 sprig of fresh sage

For the Dressing	1 tablespoonful of vegetable oil
	3 dessertspoonfuls of raspberry vinegar
	1/4 pt/150 ml red wine
	a clove of garlic
	salt
	assorted lettuce leaves
	croutons

Preparation

The first stage is to prepare the duck legs to a point where they can be stored indefinitely in the fridge.

Take a large heavy based pan and place all the confit ingredients in it. Bring very slowly to simmering point and cook for 1 hr - 1.5 hrs until the flavours are well infused and the duck legs are tender. Allow to cool fully. Because we only want the minimum of bone, leaving just the leg and thigh bone in place, trim and remove all other bones. If you intend to store the duck legs, place them in a sterilised and warmed Le Parfait jar, reheat the fat, pour over and seal.

Method

If you intend to serve the dish straight away, transfer the legs to an uncovered oven dish and cook for 15 minutes at gas mark 6/400 degrees until warmed through.

Prepare and arrange the salad - see page 31. Crush the garlic with a little salt. All that remains is to fry off the legs, skin downwards, in a the vegetable oil until very crisp. Now turn the legs over so that the skin is uppermost and continue to make the warm dressing in the pan by adding the garlic, vinegar, red wine and salt. Reduce whilst agitating the pan over the flame.

Serve the legs on the waiting lettuce leaves and complete by pouring over the warm dressing and sprinkling with croutons.

A WARM SALAD OF SCALLOPS AND BACON

To serve 4

8 fresh scallops
8 rashers of smoked streaky bacon
1 dessertspoonful of olive oil
1 oz/25 grms butter
2 dessertspoonfuls of white wine vinegar
a small glass of white wine
a small glass of dry vermouth
1 shallot or half a clove of garlic
a sprig of fresh dill
freshly ground black pepper
assorted lettuce leaves
croutons

Preparation

Ask your fishmonger to clean and trim the scallops discarding the shells.
Slice them through horizontally.   Finely chop the shallot or garlic and the dill.
Grill the bacon until crisp and roughly crumble.

Method

Prepare and arrange the salad - see page 31. Melt the butter over a medium
heat and toss in the chopped shallot.   Continue to cook until just golden and
tip in the scallops with the garlic if you are using this rather than a shallot.
Cook for a minute or so until the scallops are firm but remember that they will
shrink rapidly so it is vital not to overcook at this stage.
The next step is to pour in the olive oil, vinegar, wine, vermouth and dill.
Cook just long enough to heat through before spooning on to the waiting salad.
Sprinkle on the crisp bacon and croutons.   Serve immediately!
You can make this dish more exotic and rich by dribbling on Hollandaise Sauce
- see recipe on page 100.

A WARM SALAD OF POACHED QUAILS EGGS WITH SPINACH

To serve 4

12 quail's eggs
1 pt/600 ml water
2 tablespoonfuls of malt vinegar
12 oz/350 grms cooked spinach
8 rashers of streaky bacon
4 oz/100 grms pine kernels
1 dessertspoonful of olive oil
freshly ground nutmeg
salt and freshly ground black pepper
croutons
Hollandaise Sauce - see page 100

Preparation
The only bit of this dish that can be carried out in advance is blending the cooked spinach with the nutmeg, olive oil, salt and black pepper. Toast the pine kernels on a baking tray with a tiny sprinkling of oil or butter. Grill the bacon until crisp and roughly crumble.

Method
Prepare and arrange the salad - see page 31. Now make the Hollandaise Sauce and leave to stand in a warm place. Heat the spinach puree in a pan before covering with a close fitting lid and setting on one side. Next bring the water and vinegar to the boil with a dash of salt in a saute pan. Now comes the ultimate test of your egg poaching skill as you crack the little eggs one by one and slip them in to the gently simmering water. Cook for 3 - 4 minutes until set but take care not to overdo the eggs as we want the yolks left runny. Lift the eggs out of the water with a slotted draining spoon and store on a warm plate until all 16 eggs are cooked.

To assemble the salad - Shape the spinach into rounds and arrange on the waiting lettuce leaves. Place the poached eggs around the spinach and pour a dribble of Hollandaise over everything. Sprinkle on the bacon, pine kernels and croutons. Serve immediately!

A WARM SALAD OF SWEETBREADS, MUSHROOMS AND BACON

To serve 4
1 lb/450 grms sweetbreads
4 oz/100 grms button mushrooms
8 rashers of smoked streaky bacon
4 oz/100 grms plain flour seasoned with salt
and black pepper

The Dressing
2 dessertspoonfuls of red wine vinegar
a small glass of white wine
a small glass of dry sherry
a little vegetable oil
finely chopped chives
salt and freshly ground black pepper
assorted lettuce leaves
croutons

Preparation
Trim the sweetbreads and coat in the seasoned flour. Grill the bacon until crisp and roughly crumble.

Method
Prepare and arrange the salad - see page 31. Heat the oil in a pan over a medium heat. Tip in the sweetbreads and cook gently for about 8 minutes until crisp. Remove and drain on kitchen paper. Keep warm. Now increase the heat and toss in the mushrooms.
Cook for 3 - 4 minutes before pouring in the vinegar, wine, sherry and seasoning. Reduce slightly.

To assemble the salad - Arrange the sweetbreads on the lettuce leaves. Pour over the mushrooms and the dressing and finish by sprinkling with crisp bacon and croutons. Serve immediately decorated with finely chopped chives.

HOT SAUSAGE SALAD WITH MUSTARD DRESSING

To serve 4 8 good sausages (these can be anything within reason but we would particularly recommend Toulouse, Lincolnshire, or Marks and Spencer's sausages).

Mustard Dressing
1 tablespoonful of Dijon mustard
3 tablespoonfuls of vegetable oil
1 dessertspoonful of red wine vinegar
a small glass of red wine
2 shallots
a sprig of oregano or thyme (depending on how herby the sausages are)
fresh ground black pepper
assorted lettuce leaves

Preparation
Finely chop the shallots and herbs.

Method
Prepare and arrange the salad - see page 31. Grill the sausages until they are crisp and much of the grease has been rendered out of them. Chop in to approximately one inch lengths and keep warm.
In a pan heat the oil and cook the shallots until golden. Stir in the vinegar, red wine and mustard and reduce for a moment before adding the herbs and black pepper. Continue to cook and tip in the chopped sausages. Heat through and spoon on to the waiting salad. Serve immediately!

Oh all ye cooks and chefs,
Oh all ye pie and pasta
makers,
    Oh all ye bread bakers
and tagliatelle tasters
Bless ye the Lord.
        Praise Him and
        Magnify Him for ever

QUAILS STUFFED WITH ORANGE AND BACON WITH BURGUNDY SAUCE

This is also delicious served cold with a little salad without the sauce

To serve 4	**4 quails - boned (available from most good supermarkets)** **4 slices of brown or white bread**
The Stuffing	**l small onion** **half a green pepper** **2 oz/50 grms streaky bacon or ham** **2 oz/50 grms cooked and peeled chestnuts** **l egg** **3 oz/75 grms fresh breadcrumbs** **the grated rind of an orange** **a little vegetable oil** **a sprig of fresh thyme** **salt and freshly ground black pepper**

The Pate

Either make the recipe below or to keep things simple and quick you could buy a 4 oz/l00 grms tin of good quality pate.

4 oz/l00 grms chicken livers
l shallot
a little vegetable oil
a small glass of cognac
a clove of garlic
salt and freshly ground black pepper

The Sauce	**1/4 pt/150 ml good chicken stock** **a glass of red wine** **a glass of port** **l red onion** **2oz/50 grms unsalted butter** **l teaspoonful of redcurrant jelly** **salt and freshly ground black pepper**

Preparation

The Stuffing - Peel and finely chop the onion. De-seed and finely chop the green pepper. Chop the bacon or ham and chestnuts.

The Pate - Trim the chicken livers of any white sinew. Peel and fincly chop the shallot and garlic. Fry the livers with the oil and garlic and shallot for 4 to 5 minutes. Flambe with the cognac. Season with salt and black pepper and process the whole lot to a smooth puree. Allow to cool.
The Toast - Toast the bread and cut out in to disks approximately 4 in. across.
The Sauce - Peel and finely chop the red onion.

Method
Preheat the oven to gas mark 7/425 degrees.
We start by making the stuffing. Fry the onion, pepper and bacon in the oil until cooked. Add in the chestnuts, orange rind, leaves of thyme, salt and pepper. Cook for a minute or two longer. Remove from the heat and allow to cool slightly. Toss in the breadcrumbs and bind everything together with the egg.

Turning our attention to the quail, fill them with the stuffing mixture, brush with a little vegetable oil, season with salt and black pepper and place on a baking tray in the top of the preheated oven. Roast for 10 to 15 minutes.

While the birds are roasting we shall make the sauce. Place the chicken stock, red wine, port, redcurrant jelly and onion in a small saucepan and bring to the boil before allowing to simmer until reduced by half. Add a little salt and black pepper. Allow to cool.

When you are ready to serve the dish, reheat the sauce, add a little more port if necessary, reduce again and finish by whisking in the butter. This gives a shine to the sauce and helps to thicken it.

To serve
Spread the pate on the toast and warm through on plates in the oven. Next position one bird on each croute, surround with the sauce and serve with some nice dark green watercress.

TERRINE OF CHICKEN LIVERS WITH PORT JELLY

To serve 6 - 8   12 oz/300 grms chicken livers
6 oz/150 grms duck breast
1/4 pt/150 ml double cream
1 egg
1 egg yolk
1 1/2 leaves of gelatine
a small glass of port
1 large clove of garlic
a little vegetable oil
salt and freshly ground black pepper

Port Jelly   1/4 pt/150 ml port
1/4 pt/150 ml orange juice
1 dessertspoonful of redcurrant jelly
2 1/2 leaves of gelatine

Equipment 6 - 8 dariole moulds 2 1/2 in. diameter x 2 1/4 in.high

Preparation
It is essential to use a food processor to prepare this dish as it is important
that the chicken livers are blended to a smooth consistency. Trim the raw
chicken livers of any white sinew. Dice the raw duck breast. Separately
soften the 1 1/2 leaves of gelatine in two separate bowls of cold water.
Lightly oil the dariole moulds. Preheat the oven to gas mark 4/300.

Method
This is a delightfully simple dish to make as the magimix does most of the
work. Commence by putting the chicken livers and garlic in to the bowl of
the magimix and whizz until smooth. Next add the egg and egg yolk, salt
and black pepper and whizz again.

In a small saucepan heat the port and drop in the softened leaves of gelatine.
 Cook for a moment until dissolved and pour this in to the chicken liver
mixture. Whizz again and pour in the cream. Give another quick whizz.
Transfer the mixture to a clean bowl and stir in the chopped duck breast
before spooning in to the dariole moulds.

These have to be cooked in a water bains-marie and the simplest way to do this is to half fill a roasting tray with hot water, stand the moulds in it and cover with tin foil taking care to tightly crimp the foil to the lip of the tray. Place in the middle of the oven for 40 to 50 minutes. This is a good opportunity to make the **Port Jelly**. To check that they are adequately cooked peel back the foil and press the top of the pates gently. They should be firm to the touch. They will however still be quite pink in the middle and this is how they should be. Remove the terrines from the water and allow to cool in the fridge.

The **Port Jelly** is made by simply melting the redcurrant jelly in to the port and orange juice in a small saucepan before adding the softened gelatine. Cook for a moment or two more before pouring to a thickness of about half an inch in a shallow tray. Allow to set (this could take up to 2 hours) before chopping up in to cubes. Store in the fridge and use to decorate the terrines.

There are many other decorations you can add but we would recommend just a little salad or watercress with spring onions and possibly some chopped truffles on top of the terrines themselves. Serve with hot toast.

HAM AND OYSTER MUSHROOM TAGLIATELLE WITH FRESH PARMESAN

To serve 4

8 oz/200 grms lean smoked ham
12 oz/300 grms fresh tagliatelle
1 oz/25 grms cheddar
6 oz/150 grms oyster mushrooms
2 oz/50 grms button mushrooms
1/4 pt/150 ml double cream
1/4 pt/150 ml creme fraiche or sour cream
1 glass of dry white wine
1 oz/25 grms knob of butter
a clove of garlic
fresh parmesan
a handful of fresh chives
salt and freshly ground black pepper

Preparation
Slice the ham in to strips. Grate the cheese. Slice the mushrooms. Crush the garlic with a little salt. Chop the chives.

Method
Put a large pan of water on to boil. Add salt and a few drops of oil.
Next take a saute pan and melt the butter before tipping in the garlic. Cook for a minute or two and add the mushrooms and ham. Continue to cook over a strong heat, stirring all the time. After 3 to 4 minutes pour in the wine and reduce a little. Stir in the cream, the creme fraiche and the cheddar and continue the reduction process for another minute or two until the sauce is smooth and creamy. Add the chives, check the seasoning and remove from the heat.

We can now allow this to stand while we cook the pasta in the boiling water. When this is drained and arranged on the warmed plates re-heat the sacue, stirring all the time and spoon on to the top. Sprinkle with fresh parmesan and serve immediately.

Variation
Clearly this dish makes an excellent main course. To make it a little less rich and expensive to prepare, the cream sauce can be made from the excellent **Bechamel Sauce** recipe that we give on page 101 and finished with cream.

FILLETS OF SALMON WITH YELLOW PEPPER AND PRAWN SAUCE

This dish never sounds as nice as it tastes. The sauce is delicate and goes beautifully with a meaty fish such as salmon.

To serve 4
    4 x 6 oz/150 grms fillets of fresh Scotch salmon cut 1 in. thick
    6 oz/150 grms good quality frozen prawns
    2 large yellow peppers
    1 pt/600 ml dry white wine
    1/4 pt/150 ml double cream
    1 dessertspoonful of white wine vinegar
    a few sprigs of fresh coriander or dill
    salt and freshly ground black pepper

Preparation
De-seed and roughly chop the peppers. Defrost the prawns reserving 4 tablespoonfuls of the juice. Finely chop the fresh herbs.

Method
Preheat the oven to gas mark 6/400 degrees. With this dish we will start on the sauce but put the salmon in the oven so that it is ready at about the same time as the sauce is completed.

We begin by making a puree of the yellow peppers by poaching them in about 1/4 pt/150 ml of the wine until soft. They should then be drained and magimixed before being passed through a sieve in to a clean saucepan.

At this stage the salmon fillets should be poached in an ovenproof dish in 1/4 pt/150ml of wine. They should be seasoned and covered with foil and placed in the top of the oven for 10 to 15 minutes.

Returning to the sauce, we should now pour in the 4 tablespoonfuls of prawn juice and 7 tablespoonfuls of wine. This should be stirred and reduced by about a quarter. Pour in the cream and reduce further. Finally tip in the prawns and the vinegar. Heat through, add the herbs and season to taste. You may need to sweeten the sauce slightly with a little sugar or Marsala.

To serve
Place the salmon fillets on warm plates and pour the sauce around or over them according to your personal preference.

SCALLOPS AND BRILL WITH TWO SAUCES

To serve 4

4 x 6 oz/150 grms fillets of brill
8 king scallops
4 oz/100 grms salted butter
the juice of a lemon
a few sprigs of fresh coriander
some puff pastry fleurons
freshly ground black pepper
1/2 pt/300 ml Choron Sauce - see page 44
1/2 pt/300 ml Beurre Blanc Sauce - see page 44

Method
This is a very simple dish as the brill should be grilled with lots of lemon juice having been brushed with a little melted butter. The scallops should be sauteed until golden, also in butter.

The appeal of the presentation is to eat two different fished and two different sauces and whilst how one chooses to present these is a matter of taste, we would recommend that you pour a little of each sauce on either side of each warmed (not hot or the sauces will separate) plate, placing the brill on the pink **Choron Sauce** and the scallops on the **Beurre Blanc Sauce**. Decorate with fresh coriander and pastry fleurons.

Choron Sauce	8 oz/225 grms salted butter
	2 heaped tablespoonfuls of peeled, seeded and chopped tomatoes
	4 fl oz/12 ml dry white wine or dry sherry
	3 egg yolks
	1 shallot
	the juice of two lemons
	1 teaspoonful of black peppercorns
	a sprig of fresh tarragon

Method

Finely chop the shallot. Puree the tomatoes. Boil the lemon juice and the wine together with the tarragon, peppercorns and shallot until reduced by half. This now becomes the basis, when strained, for the sauce. Transfer to a bains-marie, return to a low heat and blend in the egg yolks with a whisk, continuing until the mixture becomes thick and slightly foaming. Remove from the heat as it is crucial not to overcook at this stage. We are now ready to add the melted butter. This should be done by pouring it in as a thin stream, whisking vigorously. You will notice a white residue at the bottom of the butter - let this go in to the sauce. Fold in the fresh tomato puree. There should be no need for further seasoning. Set aside, keeping the sauce at kitchen temperature. Serve as soon as possible.

Beurre Blanc Sauce

	6 - 7 oz/150 - 175 grms unsalted butter - cold from the fridge
	3 tablespoonfuls double cream
	3 shallots - finely chopped
	2 tablespoonfuls of white wine vinegar
	3 tablespoonfuls of dry white wine
	salt and freshly ground black pepper
	a little lemon juice

Method

In a heavy based pan cook the shallots in the wine and vinegar until the liquor is reduced to about one tablespoonful. Remove from the heat and add 2 tablespoonfuls of cold water and 3 tablespoonfuls of double cream. Just before serving put the pan back on a low heat, whisk the cold butter into the sauce in knobs and heat through but do not allow to boil. Season with salt, black pepper and lemon juice.

SOLE IN LETTUCE WITH SCALLOP MOUSSELINE

To serve 4	2 lemon sole weighing 8 - 10 oz/250 grms - filleted 4 large lettuce leaves 1 oz/25 grms salted butter 1/2 pt/300 ml Hollandaise Sauce - see page
For decoration	4 large scallops 1 oz/25 grms unsalted butter
The Scallop Mousseline	6 oz/125 grms scallops 1 egg 9 fl oz/250 ml double cream a sprig of fresh dill salt and freshly ground white pepper
Equipment	4 x 3 in. diameter ramekins

Preparation

Blanch the lettuce leaves in a little salted boiling water just long enough for them to become soft. Drain on a clean tea towel. Butter the ramekins. Trim the scallops.

Method

The general idea with this dish is to line the ramekins with the lettuce leaves followed by the fish fillets and finish by pouring in the mousseline mixture. All that then remains is to fold over the lettuce leaves before poaching in a bains-marie.

The first stage - lining the buttered ramekins with the leaves needs to be done with gentleness and care as you must push the leaves well in to the corners of the ramekins without breaking them. Next arrange the fillets - two to a ramekin - so that they line the walls.

Turning our attention to the mousseline mixture. This could not be simpler. Take the trimmed scallops and puree them in a food processor with the egg, salt and pepper. Once smooth fold in the cream. That's it! All that remains is to pour the mixture in to the middle of the waiting ramekins and finish by folding over the lettuce leaves.

When the time comes to serve, heat the oven to gas mark 6/400 degrees, make a bains-marie by pouring sufficient hot water in to a roasting tray to come half way up the sides of the ramekins. Cover the whole thing with foil and poach for 25 to 30 minutes until firm to the touch. Next remove the ramekins and gently turn out the contents on to some kitchen roll to absorb any excess liquid. Serve each one in the centre of a warmed plate surrounded by Hollandaise Sauce and decorate with a scallop that should be fried in butter until golden and thinly sliced.

RED MULLET WITH SUN-DRIED TOMATOES

To serve 4   8 small red mullet
                    2 tablespoonfuls of olive oil

The Sauce   6 English tomatoes
                    4 sun-dried tomatoes
                    2 tablespoonfuls of olive oil
                    3 shallots
                    2 cloves of garlic
                    1/2 pt/300 ml dry white wine
                    1 dessertspoonful of tomato puree
                    the juice of a lemon
                    a pinch of sugar
                    a pinch of Herbes de Provence
                    salt and freshly ground black pepper

Preparation
Officianados of the red mullet prefer them small, ungutted and with their
scales left on. This does not mean that you cannot buy larger ones and ask
your fishmonger to gut and descale them if you prefer.

Peel and roughly chop the garlic and shallots. Peel and de-seed the
tomatoes. Chop the sun-dried tomatoes.

Method
We will make the sauce first. Heat the olive oil in a saute pan and cook the
garlic and shallots until soft. Toss in the fresh and sun-dried tomatoes, white
wine and Herbes de Provence. Cook over a brisk heat to reduce, adding
lemon juice, sugar and tomato puree. Continue to cook until the fluid is
reduced by half. Season to taste and remove from the heat.

Turning our attention to the fish. These can be grilled, fried or, nicest of all,
barbecued over charcoal with sprigs of fresh rosemary. In any event the
fish should be scored two or three times diagonally across each side and
brushed with olive oil. Cook for around 10 minutes each side depending on
their size and the heat of your fire. Test with a skewer the tip of which
should be pressed to the middle of the fish and should feel hot. Reheat the
sauce and serve the mullet with watercress and saute potatoes.

SALMON AND ASPARAGUS IN FILO WITH HOLLANDAISE

To serve 4

4 x 6 oz/150 grms fillets of fresh Scotch salmon
4 leaves of fresh sorrel
4 large sticks of fresh asparagus
1/2 pt/300ml Hollandaise Sauce - see page 100
4 sheets of filo pastry
2 oz/50 grms unsalted butter
1 egg
half a cup of milk
salt and freshly ground black pepper

Preparation

Trim the asparagus and cut each stick to the length of each fillet. Blanch the leaves of sorrel in boiling salted water until just soft and drain on kitchen paper. Blanch and drain the asparagus in the same way. Melt the butter. Make the egg wash by beating the egg in to the milk. Butter a baking tray.

Method

Preheat the oven to gas mark 7/425 degrees. Take a large heavy based saute pan and heat up the oil. Seal the salmon on both sides and season.

To assemble the dish

We need double thickness filo pastry for this dish and we do this by brushing the pastry with the melted butter and folding over. Prepare the four sheets in this way and place one fillet of salmon wrapped in a sorrel leaf across the corner of each. Arrange the stick of asparagus on top and then gently wrap the fish up in the pastry as if you were wrapping fish and chips in newspaper, making as neat a parcel as possible. Seal with egg wash and place, seam downwards, on the buttered baking tray. Egg wash the top and bake in the middle of the oven for 15 minutes until the pastry is golden and shiny. Serve with **Hollandaise Sauce see page 100**

MONKFISH WITH MUSHROOM AND VERMOUTH SAUCE

To serve 4   1 1/2 lb/675 grms monkfish - skinned and
                                filleted
                    1 oz/25 grms unsalted butter
                    1 tablespoonful of olive oil

The Sauce   4 oz/100 grms button mushrooms
                    1 small head of fennel
                    1/2 pt/300 ml fish stock
                    1/4 pt/150 ml double cream
                    2 oz/50 grms unsalted butter
                    2 glasses of Noilly Prat
                    a few sprigs of fresh dill
                    salt and freshly ground black pepper

Preparation

Finely chop the fennel. Finely slice the mushrooms.

Method

Take a heavy based saute pan and heat the oil and the 1 oz/25 grms of butter.
Cook the monkfish over a brisk heat so that it is somewhat more than just
sealed but not fully cooked. Remove from the pan and set aside.

We now continue to make the sauce in the same pan by adding the fennel
and mushrooms and cooking until soft. Pour in the Noilly Prat and stock and
reduce by half. Now add the dill with some salt and black pepper. Pour in
the cream, return to the boil briefly before whisking in the butter. Bring back
the monkfish and carefully place them in the sauce. Continue to simmer for
2 to 3 minutes and serve with something like green beans, mange-tout or
broccoli.

MEDALLIONS OF FILLET STEAK WITH WILD MUSHROOM SAUCE

To serve 4   For each person you will need **3 x 2 oz/50 grms medallions cut from the thinner end of the fillet of Scotch beef**

The Sauce   **1/4 pt/150 ml espagnole sauce - see page 102**
                                     **1/2 pt/300 ml chicken stock or Fond de Veau
in tins from the best delicatessens
1 small wine glass of dry sherry
4 - 5 fl oz/100 - 125 ml double cream
1 oz/50 grms dried cepes or 3 oz/75 grms fresh
wild mushrooms
a little vegetable oil
salt and freshly ground black pepper**

Preparation
If you are using cepes soak them in boiling water for 20 to 30 minutes.

Method
The very great majority of sauces at the Hungry Monk are made to order.
However this is a sauce that can be made in advance - in any event it should
be made before you cook the meat. Start by taking a heavy saute pan and
bringing together the espagnole sauce, the stock and the mushrooms. Cook
over a fairly strong heat for about 4 minutes to reduce. Add the sherry and
continue to reduce for another 3 minutes before tipping in the cream and
reducing for a little longer. Taste and adjust the seasoning. Do not be afraid
to add a little bit more sherry at this stage. The sauce can now be poured in
to a warm jug and kept while the meat is sauteed.

To cook the meat first heat the pan until the oil is very hot. Introduce the
medallions, sealing both sides quickly and then continue to cook for as long as
you like your meat to be well done. If you want the medallions to be rare a
minute or two on each side should be ample.

To serve
Pour the sauce on to each plate first and position the medallions on top. If
you prefer your meat well done you may like to finish the cooking of the
medallions in the wild mushroom sauce to keep the meat moist.

FEUILLETE OF BEEF WITH OYSTERS

To serve 4 to 6

1 1/2 lbs - 2 lbs/675 grms - 900 grms rump
    steak - trimmed and cut in to 3/4 in. cubes
8 - 10 oysters - opened and cleaned
13 oz/350 grms block of frozen puff pastry -
    defrosted
4 oz/100 grms seasoned flour
6 oz/150 grms baby carrots
4 oz/100 grms button mushrooms
2 tablespoonfuls of vegetable oil
1/2 pt/300 ml chicken stock
1 pt/600 ml Guinness
1 glass of port
1 large onion
2 cloves of garlic
1 tablespoonful of sesame seeds
1 egg
half a cup of milk
salt and freshly ground black pepper

Preparation

Peel and finely chop the onion. Crush the garlic with a little salt. Wash and trim the carrots. Beat the egg in to the milk to make an egg wash. Roll the meat in the seasoned flour. Preheat the oven to gas mark 6/400 degrees.

Method

Take a heavy based saute pan. Heat the oil and fry off the onions, garlic and mushrooms for 3 to 4 minutes before transferring to a stew pot, retaining the oil for the next stage.

Fry the cubes of seasoned beef over a very hot flame to seal all sides. Also transfer these to the stew pot. Pour the port, Guinness and stock in to the saute pan, bring sharply to the boil, scraping the sides of the pan, before pouring over the meat in the stew pot.

Position the stew pot over a high flame and bring to the boil, stirring from time to time. Then allow to simmer for 10 minutes before covering and placing in the middle of the oven. Cook for 30 minutes and remove from the oven to allow the carrots to be added. Return to the oven for 10 minutes.

While the beef is stewing make the feuillete by rolling out the puff pastry to a rectangle approximately 12 in. x 18 in. Brush with egg wash, score diagonally with a fork and sprinkle with the sesame seeds. Cut in to six pieces 4 in. x 6 in. and place on a baking tray in the top of the oven for the last 10 minutes that the stew is cooking.

All that remains is to remove the stew from the oven and gently stir in the oysters with their juice. Replace the lid and allow to stand in a warm place for 10 minutes.

Assembly
The puff pastry rectangles will have risen to a sufficient height to allow you to slice each one in half horizontally with the object being to place the bottom half on each plate, spoon over the stew and top with the other half, giving the appearance of something slightly akin to a very juicy beef millefeuille. This is jolly nice with broccoli and new potatoes.

ROAST SIRLOIN WITH GARLIC, SHALLOTS AND RED WINE

To serve 4 - 6

4 1/2 lb/2 kilos sirloin - boned but not rolled
6 shallots
3 cloves of garlic
3 tablespoonfuls of olive oil
1/2 bottle of strong red wine
salt and freshly ground black pepper

Preparation
Preheat the oven to gas mark 7/425 degrees. Peel and chop in half the shallots. Peel and roughly chop the garlic.

Method
Take a roasting tin and make a bed of the garlic. Place the beef on top, pour the olive oil over and place in the top of the preheated oven for 20 minutes. Remove from the oven, baste the meat, pour over the red wine, sprinkle the shallots around the joint. Season liberally with black pepper and some salt. Return to the oven for another 20 minutes, basting at 5 minute intervals.

After 40 minutes total cooking time the meat should be cooked to the point where it is still nice and pink in the middle. Remove the meat with the shallots on to a warm serving dish and allow to rest in a warm place for 5 minutes. Pour the juices of the roasting tray in to a warm jug and serve with the meat.

Because some joints give off a lot more juice than others you will have to judge whether you have sufficient gravy. You can always increase the amount by adding more red wine and some stock and then reducing in the roasting tray over a high flame, adjusting the seasoning as you go.

FILLET OF LAMB IN FILO WITH PESTO AND ROSEMARY SAUCE

To serve 4
2 x best ends of English lamb with the eye of
    the meat filletted out
4 sheets of filo pastry
6 oz/150 grms melted butter
l egg
half a cup of milk

The Pesto
4 oz/100 grms grated parmesan
4 oz/100 grms pine kernels
1/4 pt/150 ml olive oil
1 clove of crushed garlic
5 sprigs of fresh basil
salt and freshly ground black pepper

The Sauce
1/2 pt/300 ml chicken stock
3 oz/75 grms butter
l glass of port
l glass of red wine
2 dessertspoonfuls of redcurrant jelly
2 tablespoonfuls of espagnole sauce- page 102
2 sprigs of young rosemary - finely chopped
salt and freshly ground black pepper

Preparation

Preheat the oven to gas mark 6/400 degrees. Make the pesto by putting all
the ingredients except for the oil in to a food processor and whizzing to a
smooth paste, finishing by pouring in the olive oil in a thin stream. Make up
the egg wash by beating the egg in to the milk.

Method

Prepare the lamb for roasting by cutting the two fillets in half. Next take
each sheet of filo pastry and brush one half with melted butter before folding
over to make a double thickness. Place one piece of lamb in the centre of
each piece of double thickness filo pastry and brush the edges of the pastry
with melted butter.

Spread some of the pesto mixture over the top of the lamb and then make four parcels by rolling up the lamb in the pastry like fish and chips. The melted butter acts as a 'glue' but it is important to ensure that the parcel is well sealed. Brush the tops with egg wash and roast for 8 minutes at the top of the oven and a further 5 to 10 minutes in the middle depending on the size of the lamb.

While this is cooking you can make the sauce by quite simply placing all the ingredients except for the butter in to a heavy based saute pan and reducing by half over a simmering heat. Finish by melting in the butter. Taste, season and add a little extra port at this stage if you so desire.

To serve
Pour the sauce around, rather than over, the lamb in pastry to keep things crisp and accompany by minty new potatoes and spinach.

RACK OF LAMB WITH FLAGEOLET BEANS AND GARLIC

To serve 4

Put your butcher on his metal by asking for 2 good-sized best ends of English Lamb each cut in half, chined and trimmed so that there is virtually nothing left but the eye of the lamb with a little fat and neatly trimmed bones, henceforward referred to as 'the rack'

> 10 oz/300 grms fresh breadcrumbs
> a little olive oil
> 2 oz/50 grms fresh parsley
> 3 tablespoonfuls of made up English mustard
> salt and freshly ground black pepper

The Sauce

> 1/2 pt/300 ml chicken stock
> 3 tablespoonfuls of espagnole sauce- page 102
> large glass of red wine
> 2 glasses of port
> 2 dessertspoonfuls of redcurrant jelly
> 8 oz/200 grms tin of flageolet beans
> 1 large clove of garlic
> 2 knobs of unsalted butter
> salt and freshly ground black pepper

Preparation
Preheat the oven to gas mark 7/425 degrees.   Chop the parsley finely and mix with the breadcrumbs, salt and pepper.   Crush the garlic with a little salt.   Rinse the beans under a cold tap and drain.

Method
Using a pastry brush generously coat the meat on all sides with the mustard. This allows you to dip the lamb in to the breadcrumbs and come up with a nice even coating.

Place the racks eye downwards on an oiled baking tray, dribble over a little olive oil and put in the top of the oven for 10 to 15 minutes depending on the size of the best ends and how you like the lamb to be cooked. It is much nicer served pink in the middle but this is of course a matter of taste.

While the lamb is roasting you can make the sauce. Take a heavy based pan and over a strong heat bring together the chicken stock, red wine, port, espagnole sauce, redcurrant jelly and garlic. Bring to the boil and then simmer for 8 minutes before adding the flageolet beans, salt and pepper and cook for another 5 to 6 minutes. Lastly add the butter to give a shine to the sauce and taste. You may feel at this stage that more port could be added.

To serve
The idea is to serve the lamb in two halves on something of a bed of flageolet beans surrounded by the sauce. This can best be achieved by using a slotted spoon to separate the flageolet beans from the sauce. Serve with **Dauphinoise Potatoes** - see below and **Red Cabbage 1991** - see page 85

Dauphinoise Potatoes

3 lbs/1.5 kilos potatoes - peeled and finely sliced
3/4 pt/450 ml single cream
4 oz./100 grms grated Gruyere
2 oz/50 grms butter
a clove of garlic crushed with a little salt
salt and freshly ground black pepper

Mix the cream, garlic, salt and black pepper in a bowl. Toss in the potatoes and coat thoroughly. Transfer to a buttered shallow ovenproof dish arranging the best slices in an overlapping pattern across the top. Brush with butter, sprinkle over the grated cheese and bake in the middle of the oven at gas mark 5/375 degrees for 1 1/2 hours until crisp and golden.

TENDERLOIN OF PORK IN PASTRY WITH APRICOT STUFFING AND BRANDY SAUCE

To serve 4

4 x 6 oz/150 grms pieces of pork tenderloin
13 oz/350 grms block of frozen puff pastry - defrosted
1 egg
half a cup of milk

The Stuffing

7 oz/175 grms dried apricots
1 onion
1 egg yolk
2 sprigs of fresh sage
a little vegetable oil
salt and freshly ground black pepper

The Sauce

8 fresh apricots or dried apricots soaked for 1 hour in a mixture of water and brandy
1/2 pt/300 ml chicken stock
1/4 pt/150 ml double cream
2 tablespoonfuls of espagnole sauce- page 102
3 tablespoonfuls of cognac
2 tablespoonfuls of apricot brandy
lemon juice
salt and freshly ground black pepper

Preparation
Trim any excess fat from the pork and make a 3 in. slot in the top of each piece of meat in to which the stuffing will be pressed. Soften the onion in the oil.

Make the stuffing by once again reaching for the indispensible food processor and blend together the onion, apricots, egg, sage and a little salt and pepper to the consistency of mince.

Cut the apricots for the sauce in half and remove the stones. Make an egg wash by beating the egg in to the milk. Preheat the oven to gas mark 5/375 degrees.

Method
Firstly cram the stuffing in to the four pork fillets. Turning our attention to the pastry, this should be divided in to four and rolled out in to pieces 7in. square. Now comes the deeply skilled bit for in order for the pastry to appear in a lattice design when cooked it must be cut with a series of slits whilst raw. These should be about 1/2in. long and 1/2in. apart in lines across the pastry but alternating as in bricklaying. This is wrapped around the meat sealing with the join under the meat and securing with egg wash. The pastry overlapping each end should simply be trimmed off and the ends brushed with egg wash. Put on a baking tray to cook for 20 to 25 minutes in the middle of the preheated oven and for 5 minutes in the top until golden. Whilst this is cooking make the sauce.

Depending on whether you are using dried or fresh apricots, your approach will be slightly different.
With dried apricots, reduce the chicken stock, brandies, espagnole sauce and the apricots in a pan by half.
With fresh apricots reduce the chicken stock, brandies and espagnole sauce on their own, adding the apricots towards the end so that they do not become too mushy. Add the cream with a little salt and pepper and return to the heat to reduce a little before adjusting the final flavour with a little more apricot brandy.

To serve
As with all dishes cooked in pastry serve the sauce around the pork so that the pastry remains crisp.

CASSOULET OF PORK AND DUCK

Wonderfully tasty and filling peasant food. Ideal after a hard day
in the fields washed down with plenty of rough red wine.

To serve 6 - 8

6 duck breasts
1 lb/450 grms dried haricot beans
2 lbs/900 grms belly of pork
12 small Toulouse sausages
12 rashers of streaky bacon
12 tomatoes
2 large onions
2 pts/1.2 litres chicken stock
3/4 pt/450 ml red wine
6 tablespoonfuls of fresh breadcrumbs mixed
with 3 tablespoonfuls of grated parmesan
2 tablespoonfuls of tomato puree
3 - 4 cloves of garlic
3 good pinches of herbes de Provence
finely chopped parsley
salt and freshly ground black pepper

Preparation

Soak the beans in cold water overnight. Slice the pork and bacon in to
1/2 in. strips. Peel and roughly chop the onions. Crush the garlic with a
little salt. Peel, de-seed and roughly chop the tomatoes. Preheat the oven to
gas mark 4/600 degrees.

Method

Drain the beans and stew in a large heavy based pan with one pint of the
stock for up to an hour until the beans are tender. In a separate pan fry the
duck breasts in a little oil, skin side down, over a low heat until the skin is
crisp. Remove from the heat. Lift out the breasts, retaining a cupful of the
duck fat, and allow to cool. Gently remove the skin which will be used later
and chop the duck meat in to slices one inch thick.

We can now commence the preparation of the Cassoulet itself by taking a
large ovenproof pot and frying, in the duck fat, the garlic, onions, bacon, pork,
sausages, and herbes de Provence until brown. Next pour in the remaining
stock, red wine, tomatoes and tomato puree and reduce by a third. Finally
tip in the beans and the duck meat, season and stir thoroughly.

Cover the pot and transfer to the middle of the oven and cook for about an hour and a half until thick but not dry.

Remove the lid, arrange the duck skin over the top and finish by liberally sprinkling over the breadcrumb and parmesan mixture. Brown under the grill and serve sprinkled with chopped parsley and accompanied by a watercress salad.

ROAST GROUSE WITH PORT AND REDCURRANT SAUCE

To serve 4

4 grouse
8 rashers of streaky bacon
1/2 pt/300 ml chicken stock
a bottle of red wine
2 glasses of port
1 tablespoonful of redcurrant jelly
3 tablespoonfuls of espagnole sauce- page 102
2 oz/50 grms butter
salt and freshly ground black pepper

Preparation
Preheat the oven to gas mark 6/400 degrees.

Method
Take a large roasting tin and position the birds so that they are not touching each other. Lay two rashers of bacon over each and pour three glasses of red wine around them with two glasses of water. Place in the top half of the oven and roast for about 30 minutes depending on the size and how well cooked you like your game. Ideally the breasts should be just pink.

To make the sauce
While the birds are cooking make the sauce by heating the chicken stock to a simmer and tipping in the redcurrant jelly, 1 glass of red wine and the port. Add the espagnole sauce and reduce by just less than half. Keep in a warm place until the grouse are cooked when the liquor from the roasting tin can be poured into the sauce. Reduce a little more and whisk in the butter, adjust the seasoning and serve around the birds with **bread sauce** - see page 101 , redcurrant jelly, game chips and **Potato and Mushroom Souffle** - see page 22 of **The Hungry Monk at Home**. (If you should be missing this vital volume in your kitchen library phone 0323 482178 for immediate dispatch!)

SADDLE OF RABBIT STUFFED WITH PRUNES AND SERVED WITH DIJON MUSTARD AND CREAM SAUCE

England is currently over-run with the purveyors of this delicious meat - pale and delicate, the saddle makes a welcome change from things like chicken and guinea fowl and is in this recipe ideally complemented by the prunes and Dijon mustard.

To serve 4	4 small saddles of rabbit - boned

The Stuffing
6 oz/150 grms dried prunes - stoned
4 rashers of streaky bacon
1 onion
1 egg
6 oz/150 grms fresh breadcrumbs
1 tablespoonful of olive oil
a clove of garlic
a small glass of brandy
the rind of one orange
a few sprigs of parsley
salt and freshly ground black pepper

The Sauce
1/2 pt/300 ml chicken stock
1/4 pt/150 ml double cream
1 glass of dry white wine
2 glasses of Madeira
1 dessertspoonful of Dijon mustard
2 teaspoonfuls of grain mustard
salt and freshly ground black pepper

Preparation

Soak the prunes overnight in hot water. Wash the saddles under cold running water, drain and pat dry. Peel and roughly chop the onion. Crush the garlic with a little salt. Chop the parsley. Roughly chop the prunes. Chop the bacon in to lardons. Grate the rind from the orange. Preheat the oven to gas mark 5/375 degrees.

Method

The stuffing is simply made in a deep pan over a medium heat. Start by softening the bacon, onion and garlic in the oil. Then add the prunes, parsley, orange rind, breadcrumbs, egg and brandy, stirring all the time. Finish with a little seasoning. Allow to cool before taking the saddles and laying them flat inside uppermost. Spoon the stuffing on to them and wrap them up in buttered tin foil like Christmas crackers. Lay them in a roasting tin and cook in the preheated oven for 20 to 25 minutes.

While the saddles are roasting make the sauce. In a heavy based pan combine the chicken stock and mustard with the Madeira and white wine. Bring to the boil and reduce by half to the consistency of single cream. Finish by stirring in the double cream. Bring carefully back to the boil, stirring continuously. Season to taste.

To serve

Remove the cooked saddles from the foil and pour the sauce over them. Serve with white cabbage cooked with a few sultanas and nutmeg and baked potatoes.

ROAST PHEASANT WITH CHESTNUT AND SHERRY SAUCE

To serve 4

2 hen pheasants
4 rashers of smoked streaky bacon
6 shallots
2 eating apples
a little olive oil
2 knobs of butter
1/2 pt/300 ml dry cider
1/4 pt/150 ml chicken stock
2 glasses of red wine
a clove of garlic
2 sprigs of thyme
salt and freshly ground black pepper

The Sauce

4 oz/100 grms chestnuts, cooked and peeled
1/4 pt/150 ml double cream
4 tablespoonfuls of espagnole sauce - page 102
2 glasses of dry sherry
chopped chives
salt and freshly ground black pepper

Preparation

Remove the legs from the pheasants with a sharp knife. Peel and halve the shallots. Peel and crush the garlic with a little salt. Remove the cores from the apples.

Method

Preheat the oven to gas mark 4/350 degrees. The idea is to cook the legs separately and for longer than the breasts so that they are really tender. Do this by taking a saute pan and heating the oil before browning the legs on all sides with the garlic and apples. Next pour in the cider and stock. Season. Bring sharply to the boil, cover and simmer for about 40 minutes until tender.

While the legs are cooking take the pheasants, place them in a roasting pan and stuff loosley with the shallots, butter and thyme. Season the birds and arrange the bacon over the breasts. Roast for about 25 minutes in the middle of the oven (after about 10 minutes pour two glasses of red wine and a glass of water around the birds).

Now the sauce - this should be made once the pheasant breasts and legs are cooked, both of which should be kept in a warm place. Take the liquor from both the roasting tray and the saute pan, pass through a sieve in to a clean saucepan and reduce by a third with the espagnole sauce, dry sherry and the chestnuts. Stir in the cream and bring to the boil. Simmer until the sauce has become thick and creamy, adding a little more sherry if necessary. Season and sprinkle in the chives.

To serve
Carve the breasts and serve in thick slices with the sauce poured over the legs. Serve with lattice game chips and **Red Cabbage 1991 - see page 85** .

VENISON WITH CASSIS AND SHALLOTS

To serve 4

4 venison steaks - choose steaks from the legs of young animals if possible and have them cut 3/4 in. to 1 in. thick.
a little olive oil

The Sauce

1/2 pt/300 ml chicken stock
3 shallots
2 tablespoonfuls of fresh or frozen blackcurrants
2 oz/50 grms butter
2 small glasses of cassis
a wine glass of red wine
3 tablespoonfuls of espagnole sauce- page 102
chopped chives
salt and freshly ground black pepper

Preparation
Peel and chop the shallots. If using fresh blackcurrants, pick them over and wash them.

Method
To make the sauce, which should be sharpish but slightly sweet in flavour, start by bringing to the boil the chicken stock with the wine and the espagnole sauce. Simmer, tip in the shallots and reduce by half. Then pour in the cassis, add the berries and continue to simmer for a few minutes. Adjust the seasoning and set to one side. Take a large frying pan and heat the oil until just smoking. Cook the steaks briskly, sealing both sides first for about 2 minutes each side. These should be cooked pink and the best way to test this is to press down on the middle of the steaks with your finger on the basis that the more well done the meat is the firmer it becomes to the touch. Finish with a generous sprinkling of black pepper and a little salt before serving in broad diagonal slices with the waiting sauce which should be reheated, whisking in a knob of butter. Sprinkle over the chopped chives.

Note
It may not be possible to buy young venison in which case the meat should be marinated for at least 12 hours to ensure tenderness. Make this marinade with equal quantities of olive oil and red wine and a spoonful of juniper berries.

GUINEA FOWL MARINATED WITH YOGHURT AND CUMIN

Spicy and aromatic - an unusual treatment of this bird that tastes interesting.

To serve 4

2 guinea fowl
10 oz/275 grms plain yoghurt
the juice of 2 lemons
2 dessertspoonfuls of ground cumin
2 -3 shakes of tabasco
a few sprigs of freshly chopped coriander
salt and freshly ground black pepper

Preparation

Joint the birds in to breasts and legs. Discard remainder of the carcass. Make diagonal slashes across the skin.

Make a marinade by combining the yoghurt, lemon juice, cumin, coriander, tabasco, salt and pepper. Immerse the meat for at least 2 hours. Preheat the barbecue or oven to gas mark 6/400 degrees.

Method

The nicest way to cook this is on a barbecue where the birds are cooked in the usual way and regularly brushed with the marinade. Alternatively they can be roasted in the oven in which case they can be surrounded by the marinade and cooked for about 30 minutes until brown on top.
Serve hot or cold with salad and new potatoes tossed in french dressing with crumbled crispy bacon.

BREAST OF DUCK WITH PASSION FRUIT AND MARSALA SAUCE

Still the only thing to have been on the Hungry Monk menu continuously for 24 years. Although we can't improve on the previous recipes for how to prepare crisp, ungreasy duckling we do believe that this is the best sauce so far. It is still fruity but less obvious than other fruit sauces.

To serve 4	2 large ducks with the legs removed 3 eating apples sprigs of fresh sage salt
Passion Fruit* and Marsala Sauce	1/4 pt/150 ml concentrated passion fruit juice 3/4 pt/450 ml chicken stock a small glass of Marsala 1 1/2 tablespoons of espagnole sauce-page 102 2 oz/50 grms butter salt and freshly ground black pepper

* It is crucial that you use only the highest quality concentrated passion fruit juice. Much of the stuff that you can buy in the supermarkets is too sweet and no good at all. If you have no luck with your local supplier you can make your own by cutting 10 passion fruit in half, scooping out the seeds and pulp and combining this juice with the juice of half a lemon.

Preparation
Preheat the oven to gas mark 6/400 degrees.

Method
Prick the skin of the duck breasts all over with a sharp fork to release the grease from under the skin during cooking. Rub well with salt to help the skin go really crisp. Place upside down in a roasting tray with no fat and set in the upper part of the oven to cook for 40 minutes to 1 hour. At the end of this time the ducks should be cooked but not yet crisp.

Allow to cool slightly and then break the carcasses in half to give you four separate breasts. Trim these so that they will look neat on the plate. Now lay the breasts, skin side up, on a bed of sliced apples and fresh sage in a roasting tin and return them to the oven to cook for a further 15 to 20 minutes until crisp.

While the duck breasts are roasting make the sauce by combining all the ingredients except for the butter and reducing down by a third. We are looking for a taste that is balanced between a sharp fruitiness and a sweetness that is always so welcome with duck. You may have to adjust the marsala or passion fruit juice accordingly. If you have used fresh passion fruit juice, pass the sauce through a sieve to remove the seeds.
Transfer to a clean saucepan and heat through, whisking in the butter to give a shine.

To serve
Lift the duck breasts out of the roasting tray and serve on warmed plates **surrounded** by the sauce (the skin will go soggy if you pour the sauce **over** the duck) and accompanied by Pommes Dauphinoise and Red Cabbage - pages 67 and 68 of Cooking with The Hungry Monk.

BREAST OF CHICKEN WITH WATERCRESS SAUCE

To serve 4

4 x breasts of chicken, skinned and boned
3 oz/75 grms smoked ham
3 oz/75 grms button mushrooms
6 oz/150 grms Philadelphia cream cheese
2 shallots
1/4 pt/150 ml water
1/4 pt/150 ml dry white wine
a little vegetable oil
a handful of fresh chives
salt and freshly ground black pepper

Watercress Sauce

2 bunches of watercress
3 oz/75 grms butter - softened
1/2 pt/300 ml chicken stock
1/2 pt/300 ml double cream
2 tablespoonfuls of bechamel sauce - see
page 101
a glass of dry white wine
a glass of dry sherry

Preparation

Peel and chop the shallots.   Fineley slice the mushrooms and the ham.
Finely chop the chives.
Make the watercress butter by cutting off the stalks and liquidising it the
leaves Add the butter and whizz to a smooth puree.   Set aside in the fridge.
Preheat the oven to gas mark 6/400 degrees.

Method

Firstly make the stuffing by frying the shallots in the oil with the mushrooms
and smoked ham.   Allow to cool.   Combine with the cream cheese and chives.
 Season.

Next take the chicken breasts and flatten them out with a rolling pin.   Place
the stuffing in equal parts and wrap the chicken meat tightly around and
position the breasts in a shallow tray surrounded by the wine and water.
Season the tops and cover with foil.   Place in the top of the oven for about 20
to 25 minutes.

74

To make the sauce

While the chicken breasts are cooking make the sauce by heating the stock, wine and sherry. Reduce by half. Stir in the bechamel sauce and cream and simmer for a few minutes to allow the sauce to thicken up. Add the watercress butter in little lumps, stirring all the time. Season. The finished sauce should be smooth and green and when poured over the chicken breasts will make a shiny coat.

(Take care when you remove the breasts from the poaching liquor to drain them thoroughly). This dish can be served with Basmati and Wild Rice - these should be cooked separately and then mixed .

Variation

You can substitute sorrel leaves for the watercress.

CALVES LIVER WITH RASPBERRY VINEGAR AND CREAM SAUCE

A delicate dish that is easily prepared and, without the sauce, not so exciting but jolly slimming!

To serve 4

1 lb 10 oz/700 grms calves liver
1/2 pt/300 ml chicken stock
1/4 pt/150 ml double cream
2 oz/50 grms butter
a little vegetable oil
a sherry glass of Madeira
2 dessertspoonfuls of raspberry vinegar
a sprig of fresh tarragon
salt and freshly ground black pepper

Preparation

Trim and cut the liver in to 8 x 1/2in slices.

Method

This is a simple dish to prepare. Heat the oil in a heavy based frying pan until just smoking and cook the liver for 2 minutes or so each side depending on how well cooked you like to eat this meat. We would recommend that you aim for pink but not bloody - definitely try and avoid overcooking as it will ruin the delicate texture. Once cooked, season, drain and keep in a warm place.

Maintaining a lively heat pour in to the pan the Madeira and raspberry vinegar, followed by the chicken stock. Reduce by a third over a simmering heat, stirring occasionally. Pour in the cream. Reduce to a coating consistency. Now taste and decide whether you would like to add a little more of the raspberry vinegar and Madeira depending how sharp you would like the taste of your sauce to be. Reduce a little longer to cook off the alcohol and end by adjusting the seasoning and adding the tarragon before returning the cooked liver and its juices to the pan and giving the whole dish another minute or so over the heat.

Serve with new potatoes or really smooth, creamy mashed potatoes and mange tout.

VEGETARIAN COUS - COUS
A welcome change for vegetarians from rice and pasta

To serve 4

12 oz/325 grms cous-cous
2 medium sized onions
3 carrots
half a red pepper
3/4 pt/450 ml vegetable stock
2 cloves of garlic
2 teaspoonfuls of hot chili powder
1 dessertspoonful of tomato puree
2 teaspoonfuls of mixed herbs
salt and freshly ground black pepper

8 tomatoes
4 sticks of celery
1 green pepper
2 parsnips
a little vegetable oil

Preparation
Peel and roughly chop the onions. Peel, de-seed and roughly chop the tomatoes. De-seed the green pepper. Chop the celery, carrots, parsnips and pepper in to 1/2 in cubes. Soak the cous-cous for ten minutes in plain warm water and set aside. Crush the garlic with a little salt.

Method
Heat the oil in a large, heavy based saucepan that has a good fitting lid. Toss in the garlic, onions and chili powder and cook without the lid until soft. Add in all the other ingredients except the cous-cous, fit on the lid and bring sharply to the boil before allowing to simmer over a medium heat for 1/2 hour - check after 15 minutes and add a little more vegetable stock if things are looking dry.

Now is the time to start steaming the cous-cous and simultaneously to remove the lid from the vegetables and allow both to cook for about 15 minutes. (A good tip for steaming cous-cous is to line a colander with a tea towel so that the little grains do not fall through the holes and cover with a lid or foil).

To serve
When the cous-cous is cooked stir in the butter and present the dish like curry with the vegetable mixture on top of the cous-cous. Accompany with a watercress salad and poppadoms.

MARINATED VEGETABLES EN BROCHETTE WITH APRICOTS

We find that vegetarians are always touched whenever anybody makes a real effort in their direction. These little kebabs can look very pretty and taste delicious.

To serve 4

1 aubergine
1 red pepper
1 green pepper
1 yellow pepper
16 button mushrooms
16 cherry tomatoes
2 courgettes
8 shallots

8 oz/200 grms Basmati Rice
1 pt/600 ml water

4 oz/100 grms Wild Rice
1 pt/600 ml water

2 tablelspoonfuls of pine kernels
2 oz/50 grms dried apricots
4 oz/100 grms butter
2 shallots
a handful of fresh chives

For the Marinade

1/2 pt/300 ml olive oil
1 dessertspoonful of Dijon mustard
1 teaspoonful of soy sauce
2 dessertspoonfuls of peanut
butter
1 tablespoonful of white wine
vinegar
1 dessertspoonful of honey
1 clove of garlic
1 level teaspoonful of ground
coriander
1 level teaspoonful of ground
cumin
salt and freshly ground black
pepper

Equipment - 8x8 in skewers

Preparation overnight
The ideal is to prepare the vegetables the day before and allow them to soak in the marinade overnight in a rectangular flat bottomed dish or roasting tin. Make the marinade by combining all the ingredients apart from the oil to a smooth consistency and then stir in the oil.

Moving on to the vegetables. It goes without saying that these all need to be in approximately one inch pieces to slide on to the skewers. The aubergine should be sweated by sprinkling with salt for 1/2 an hour, rinsed in cold water and patted dry. The shallots should be peeled and split in half, the peppers de-seeded.

Now the fun bit - pushing the vegetables on to the skewers so that each person gets a fair selection. Give the marinade a final stir and lay the kebabs side by side, giving them a turn each to ensure that they are thoroughly coated. Leave overnight, turning again from time to time (this does not mean however that you have got to stagger out of bed at three in the morning to give the kebabs a turn!).

Preparation the following day
Boil the wild rice with a little salt and the water until all the water has evaporated and if the rice is cooked it will be splitting out of its brown outer case. Don't be afraid to add a little more water and cook for longer if necessary. Drain and set aside.

With the Basmati rice start by thoroughly rinsing it under a cold running tap. Next peel and chop the challots and chop the apricots. Toss them with the butter in to a heavy based pan that has a tightly fitting lid. Fry until soft and tip in the rice. Cook over a fairly high heat, stirring all the time for about 2 or 3 minutes before pouring in the water. Add a pinch of salt and bring to the boil before simmering over a very low heat with the lid on for 10 minutes. Stir, replace the lid and cook for a further 5 minutes. Set aside.

While this is cooking toast the pine kernels under the grill with a little oil.

Method
Heat up the grill. Position the kebabs on a baking tray that will fit under the grill. Sprinkle with freshly ground black pepper and cook for 3 minutes or so each side. Meanwhile reheat the rice by steaming.

To serve
Position the rice in concentric rings, sprinkle with chopped chives and the pine kernels and finish by laying the kebabs across. Serve with apricot or mango chutney and a dressed green salad.

SPINACH AND GRUYERE SOUFFLE WITH SWEET PEPPER SAUCE

To serve 2 as a main course or 4 as a starter.

1 lb/450 grms fresh spinach or
8 oz/225 grms frozen spinach
2 oz/50 grms Gruyere
2 oz/50 grms butter
2 oz/50 grms plain flour
1/2 pt/300 ml milk
4 eggs
2 extra whites
1 tablespoonful of chopped parsley
salt
freshly ground black pepper
Grated nutmeg

Sweet PepperSauce

4 large red peppers
1/4 pt/150 ml water
1/4 pt/150 ml double cream
a glass of dry white wine
a glass of dry sherry
salt
freshly ground black pepper

Equipment -   **a 2 pt/1.2 litre souffle dish - buttered**

Preparation

First we must make the sauce.   De-seed and roughly chop the peppers.
Take a large heavy based pan with a tightly fitting lid.   Pour in the water
and wine and add the peppers.   Bring to the boil, cover and simmer for
about 5 minutes until the peppers are tender.   Transfer them with their
liquor to a liquidiser and process until smooth.   Pass through a sieve and
pour the strained juice in to a clean saucepan.   Add the cream and sherry
and simmer, stirring from time to time until you have achieved a smooth
coating consistency.   Season to taste and set aside.

Separate the eggs. Grate the cheese. If using fresh spinach, wash it in several changes of water, remove the tough stalks, roughly chop it and cook it until soft with only the water still clinging to the leaves. If you are using frozen spinach just cook it carefully without any water. Dry the cooked spinach by first draining it and then rolling it up in a fresh dry tea towel and squeezing out the excess moisture. Warm the milk. Preheat the oven to gas mark 6/400 degrees.

Method
We are now going to make a thick bechamel sauce. Melt the butter in a large pan, tip in the flour and stir to form a roux. Cook for 3 to 4 minutes before slowly whisking in the warmed milk. Bring to the boil and simmer for 5 minutes stirring all the time. Set aside and sprinkle on the grated Gruyere. Stir in the spinach and allow to cool slightly.

Whisk the egg whites with a balloon whisk to form stiff peaks. Stir the egg yolks in to the cooled spinach mixture and follow this by stirring in one third of the whisked egg whites. Remembering that we want this souffle to be as light and airy as possible the next procedure is to pour the spinach mixture over the remaining egg whites and using a spatula, fold in quickly with figure of eight movements until the mixture is just uniform in colour but no more.

Transfer the mixture to the buttered souffle dish and place in the oven on a baking sheet for approximately 30 minutes. It iss a matter of taste how well cooked you like the souffle - obviously the less you cook it the creamier it will be.

To serve
Spoon on to hot plates immediately and half cover with Sweet Pepper Sauce.

ARTICHOKE DAUPHINOISE

To serve 4 as an accompaniment or 2 as a vegetarian main course

2 1/2 lbs/1.25 kilos Jerusalem artichokes
1/2 pt/300 ml double cream
1/4 pt/300 ml milk
2 cloves of garlic crushed with a little salt
4 oz/100 grms butter
4 oz/100 grms grated Gruyere
salt and freshly ground black pepper

Method
Commence by preheating the oven to gas mark 5/375 degrees and scrubbing the artichokes thoroughly. Next slice the vegetables and lay them in a buttered rectangular ovenproof dish interleaved with knobs of butter and crushed garlic. Pour over the milk and cream together, sprinkle with salt and plenty of freshly ground black pepper before topping with the grated Gruyere. Bake in the middle of the oven for 30 to 40 minutes until golden brown.

BRUSSELS SPROUTS WITH BACON AND CHESTNUTS

To serve 4

1 lb/450 grms Brussels sprouts
8 rashers of streaky bacon - chopped
6 oz/150 grms chestnuts - peeled, cooked and chopped (the vacuum packed variety)
2 oz/50 grms unsalted butter
salt and freshly ground black pepper

Method
Trim and blanch the sprouts in boiling salty water for 2 to 3 minutes. Drain and reserve. In a deep saute pan melt the butter and cook the bacon and chestnuts until the bacon is crisp. Turn off the heat. Tip in the sprouts and stir gently until everything is well mixed and transfer to an ovenproof dish. The sprouts may need a minute or two more cooking in the oven before serving depending on how crisp you like your vegetables. If you have a joint roasting in the oven a nice idea is to sprinkle the chestnuts around it during the last 10 minutes of cooking before mixing them in with the sprouts.

CELERIAC PUREE

To serve 4
1 1/2 lbs/675 grms celeriac
1/2 pt/300 ml dry white wine
8 oz/200 grms butter
1/4 pt/150 ml double cream
salt and freshly ground black pepper

Method
Peel and chop the celeriac and put in to a saucepan with the white wine, butter, salt and pepper. Bring to the boil, cover and simmer until soft - anything from 10 to 20 minutes. Lift out the celeriac with a slotted spoon and put in to a liquidiser with the cream and whizz to a smooth puree. Transfer to an ovenproof dish and warm through for a few minutes before serving.

DEE'S CABBAGE

To serve 4
1 large Savoy cabbage - sliced
4 shallots - peeled and finely chopped
1 oz/25 grms butter
1/4 pt/150 ml double cream
finely chopped parsley
salt, freshly ground black pepper and nutmeg

Method
Put a large saucepan of salty water on to boil. While this is happening melt the butter in a saute pan and cook the shallots until soft before stirring in the double cream, nutmeg, salt and pepper. Take off the heat.
Returning our attention to the boiling salty water we should now tip in the cabbage and blanch it for a minute or two, bearing in mind that this really does cook very quickly indeed. All that remains is to drain the cabbage, transfer it to a warm serving dish and pour over the cream and shallot sauce. Toss. Finish by sprinkling some chopped parsley on the top.

RED CABBAGE 1991

To serve 6

1 x 5 in. diameter red cabbage
1 medium onion
2 apples
6 oz/150 grms sultanas
1 teaspoonful of ground cumin
1 teaspoonful of ground juniper berries
1 teaspoonful of caraway seeds
2 tablespoonfuls of vegetable oil
2 tablespoonfuls of red wine vinegar
1 tablespoonful of brown sugar
1/2 pt/300 ml red wine
salt and freshly ground black pepper

Method

Commence by cutting the cabbage into slices the thickness of medium sliced bread. Next peel, chop and puree the onions and apples with the red wine in a liquidiser. Take a large heavy based pan and toss in the cabbage with the apple and onion puree followed by all the other ingredients. Go easy on the salt at this stage. Mix all the ingredients thoroughly and place the pan over a high heat. Bring to the boil, cover and simmer for about 30 minutes taking great care not to allow things to boil dry and burn as this will ruin everything. When you start you may think that there is not enough liquid, however the cabbage, given time, produces its own juice and provided you take things reasonably gently it should not be necessary to add any more liquid. It is essential to finish by tasting the cabbage and if necessary adjusting the sugar or salt and the vinegar. Drain and transfer in to a warm serving dish.

BAKED LEMON TART WITH BLACKCURRANT SAUCE

Very pure, very lemony - ideal at the end of a rich dinner.

To serve 4   **8 oz/225 grms rich shortcrust pastry- (see page 13 for recipe substituting half teaspoonful of caster sugar for the pinch of salt)**

2 eggs
7 1/2 fl oz/225 ml double cream
2 dessertspoonfuls of caster sugar
the zest and juice of 1 1/2 lemons
a little icing sugar

Equipment   **4 x 4in. diameter, loose-bottomed tart tins.**

Preparation

Preheat the oven to gas mark 6/400 degrees. Bake blind the four pastry cases as described on page 92 and set aside. Turn the oven down to gas mark 5/375 degrees.

Method

Bring together in a bowl the lemon juice, zest and caster sugar and stir. Next tip in the cream followed by the eggs and whisk until the mixture is an even consistency with the eggs fully broken down. Pour in to the waiting pastry cases and place on a baking tray in the middle of the oven for 30 minutes until set.

This would be a good moment to make a fruit sauce - ideally blackcurrant - by simply cooking the fruit with a little water and as much sugar as your taste prefers. Follow by pureeing and sieving. Serve chilled.

Back to the tarts. These should be kept in a cool place until the time has come for them to be eaten when they should be returned to the oven for a few minutes to crisp up the pastry. Finish by sprinkling a little sieved icing sugar on the top and surround with the Blackcurrant Sauce.

ALMOND AND APRICOT ROULADE WITH APRICOT SAUCE

A distant relative of the Swiss Roll - this moist Almond Roulade is filled with whipped cream and chopped apricots.

To serve 6

The Roulade	4 oz/100 grms flaked almonds
	2 oz/50 grms caster sugar
	3 eggs - separated
	1/2 pt/300 ml double cream
	1 lb/450 grms tinned apricots
	1 tablespoonful of caster sugar
	the grated rind of half a lemon
	a small glass of apricot brandy
The Sauce	1 lb/450 grms tinned apricots
	lemon juice
Equipment	13 in. x 9 in. Swiss roll baking tin

Preparation
Preheat the oven to gas mark 5/375 degrees. Oil and line the baking tin with greaseproof paper. Drain and roughly chop the apricots and whip the cream.

Method
We will start by making the almond base that will later be rolled up. For some reason this pudding works better when you grind your own almonds by putting flaked almonds and 2 oz/50 grms caster sugar in to a Magimix than it does by using ready prepared ground almonds. Once you have done this whisk the egg whites to soft peaks and fold in the lemon rind, egg yolks and almond mixture. Spread this evenly on to the prepared baking tray and cook in the top of the oven for 12 to 15 minutes to a point where the roulade base is just brown and slightly springy - to overcook will make things too dry. Remove from the oven and allow to half cool in its tin before covering with a just damp tea towel and leaving to cool completely.

Next take a sheet of greaseproof paper slightly larger than the roulade base and sprinkle with the tablespoonful of caster sugar. On to this place the roulade base face down and lift away the baking tin to reveal the oily paper. This must be peeled away with some care.

Now sprinkle the base with the apricot brandy and spread the whipped cream evenly over the whole surface area, leaving a half inch border clear each end. Sprinkle the chopped apricots in to the cream.

Now comes the moment when you demonstrate your extreme skill as a pudding cook! Position the roulade in a portrait rather than a landscape orientation in front of you and take hold of the greaseproof paper under the edge furthest from you and gently pull up and towards you. The idea is that the roulade will roll like a thick carpet as the paper is pulled forward but it will be necessary to help get it started by folding over the top edge.

Transfer the roulade to a long dish and serve in thick slices with the **Apricot Sauce**. This is made by simply removing and draining the apricots from the second tin, reserving approximately half the syrup and liquidising the fruit to a smooth consistency with the syrup. Add a little lemon juice. The roulade and sauce is nicer when served chilled from the fridge.

LAYERED CHOCOLATE MOUSSE CAKE

To serve 8

The Sponge
3 oz/75 grms caster sugar   3 eggs
2 oz/50 grms plain flour   1 oz/12 grms cocoa powder
1 oz/12 grms melted unsalted butter

The Dark Chocolate Mousse
3 oz/75 grms dark chocolate   1/2 pt/300 ml double cream

The White Chocolate Mousse
3 oz/75 grms white chocolate   1/4 pt/150 ml double cream

The Syrup
4 tablespoonfuls of rum   1 tablespoonful of caster sugar
3 tablespoonfuls of water

The Decoration
8 oz/225 grms dark chocolate   1/2 pt/300 ml double cream

Equipment   7 in. diameter 3 1/2 in. deep round,
loose-bottomed cake tin

Preparation
At first sight this pudding looks frightfully complicated but in fact what we are making is something that has layers of chocolate sponge interleaved with layers of dark and white chocolate mousse. This is served in thick slices with the rum syrup.

Before we can do anything we have to make the sponge. Preheat the oven to gas mark 5/375 degrees. Line the bottom of the cake tin with greaseproof paper and liberally butter the sides. In a large bowl whisk the eggs and sugar together either using an electric hand held whisk or a Kenwood or a non-mechanical balloon whisk over a pan of gently simmering water. Whisk until the mixture is thick and creamy and holds the imprint of the whisk when it is drawn across the surface.

Lightly fold in the sieved flour and cocoa powder followed by the cooled melted butter and spoon in to the waiting cake tin. Bake in the middle of the oven for about 15 minutes. Test that the cake is cooked by pressing the top gently - it should spring back up. Remove from the oven and allow to stand for a minute or two before turning out on to a wire cooling rack. Finally wash the cake tin and line it with two broad strips of greaseproof paper laid at right angles ot each other with enough hanging over the edge so that when later you come to lift out your creation you can do so without tears.

To make the syrup - combine all the ingredients and leave to stand.

Method
We shall make the two mousses simultaneously in separate bain-maries on the top of the stove. While the dark chocolate is melting in one and the white chocolate is melting in the other whip the two amounts of double cream in separate bowls until stiffish. Allow the molten chocolate to cool . This is a good moment to cut the cake in to three layers of equal thickness returning the bottom layer to the cake tin.

Now back to the whipped cream - fold in the chocolate taking care to lose as little of the air in the whipped cream as possible.

Next the fun bit! Brush the layer of cake already in the tin with some of the rum syrup and spoon in the dark mousse. Allow to stand and set in the fridge for 10 minutes before repeating the process with another layer of cake and the white mousse mixture. Back to the fridge for another 10 minutes before placing the final layer of sponge on the top, remembering to brush this with syrup on its underside. Return the whole cake to the fridge for three hours to set thoroughly.

Lift out and position on a cake board in readiness for decorating with chocolate ganache. This is easily made by melting the dark chocolate and whisking in the double cream. Allow to cool to a point where the chocolate mixture is the considtency of chocolate spread and coat the layer cake using a palette knife.

The whole caboodle can now be put in the fridge for 30 to 40 minutes so that the icing can set properly. Finally transfer to a pretty plate and serve in thick slices with either plain pouring cream or cream flavoured with a little instant coffee and caster sugar.

TROPICAL FRUIT BRULEE TART

To serve 4

The Pastry
4 1/2 oz/110 grms plain flour
2 oz/50 grms icing sugar
3 1/2 oz/85 grms unsalted butter
1 egg yolk
2 drops of vanilla essence
a pinch of salt

The Brulee
1/2 pt/300 ml double cream
3 egg yolks
2 oz/50 grms caster sugar
2 drops of vanilla essence

a selection of thinly sliced tropical fruit
1 tablespoonful of apricot jam
1 tablespoonful of caster sugar

Equipment -
4 x 4in. diameter x 3/4 in. deep,
loose-bottomed tart tins.

Preparation
Preheat the oven to gas mark 6/400 degrees. We need to fully bake blind the tart cases using pastry made in the following way. Mix the flour, icing sugar, vanilla essence and salt. Rub in the butter and combine everything together with the egg yolk. Allow this to rest in the fridge for at least 45 minutes before attempting to roll it out. Remember when baking blind to line the raw pastry with greaseproof paper and baking beans or dried haricot beans. Cook on a baking tray in the top of the oven for 8 to 10 minutes with the last couple of minutes being without the paper and beans to allow things to crisp.

Turning our attention to the brulee mixture we need a very low oven of no more than gas mark 2/300 degrees. The mixture for this is made by putting the egg yolk, sugar and vanilla essence in to a bowl and whisking together. Then bring the cream to the boil in a little saucepan and pour in to the egg yolk mixture, whisking all the time. You now have a brulee mixture which needs to be baked for 45 minutes in an ovenproof dish set in a roasting tray of hot water with everything covered by tin foil. Lift out and allow to cool.

Assembly

We have the cases and we have the cream custard. All that remains is to spoon the one in to the other and decorate the tops with the tropical fruit. Done carefully this can be very attractive and although we have suggested tropical fruits there is no reason why you should not include summer fruits from the garden such as raspberries and strawberries.

What makes the whole thing compulsively delicious is the finishing touch in which you thinly spread strained apricot jam over the top and sprinkle with caster sugar before flashing under a preheated grill at medium heat for long enough to see the sugar caramelise. Watch this carefully so that the brulees do not burn. It would do no harm to accompany this with a little **Apricot Sauce** .

TREACLE PUDDING WITH ORANGE CUSTARD

To serve 6

3 oz/75 grms plain flour
3 oz/75 grms self-raising flour
2 oz/50 grms caster sugar
1/2 oz/12 grms baking powder
1 egg
1/4 pt/150 ml milk
3 oz/75 grms suet
1 lb/450 grms golden syrup
the grated zest of a lemon

Equipment   6 x 1/4 pt/150 ml pudding basins with lids or
greaseproof paper and tin foil tied on with string.

Method

This is a delightfully simple pudding and need not be heavy and stodgy.
Mix the egg and milk together.   Place all the ingredients except for the
golden syrup, milk and egg in to a mixing bowl.   Stir together and make a
well in the middle.   Pour in the egg and milk mixture and using a wooden
spoon stir round and round in the middle of the bowl so that the dry
ingredients gradually become incorporated without going lumpy.

Turning our attention to the pudding basins pour golden syrup in the
bottom of each to a depth of 3/4 in and top up with the suet mixture.
Seal tightly and cook for 40 to 45 minutes in a steamer.   Turn out upside
down and serve warm with **Home-made orange custard-**

6 egg yolks   3 oz/75 grms caster sugar
3/4 pt/450 ml milk   the zest of an orange
                                     a vanilla pod

Method

Start by mixing the caster sugar and egg yolks in a bowl.   In a saucepan
heat the milk with the vanilla pod and the zest of orange and allow to stand
for a few minutes for the flavours to infuse.   Lift out the vanilla pod and
pour the milk on to the egg yoks and sugar, stirring with a wooden spoon.
Return the whole lot to the saucepan and over a medium heat, cook, stirring
all the time.   The penalty for not stirring is scrambled egg!
Continue to cook until the custard is of a coating consistency.   You can tell
this by seeing if the custard will coat the back of the wooden spoon in such
a way that if you drag your finger across it it will leave a clear line.   At this
point the custard is cooked and should be kept in a warm place.

COCONUT AND PISTACHIO ICE CREAM

To make about half a gallon of ice cream

4 eggs
1 pt/600 ml double cream
3 oz/75 grms caster sugar
1 x 1 lb/425 grms of sweetened coconut cream
4 oz/100 grms unsalted pistachio nuts
a glass of Malibu or white rum

Method
Peel and halve the nuts. Whisk the eggs and sugar together in a bowl set over a pan of boiling water until thick enough to hold the imprint of the whisk. Remove from the heat and allow to cool completely. In a separate bowl whip the cream to soft peaks. All that remains is to fold together the eggs, cream, nuts, coconut cream and Malibu or rum, taking care to lose as little of the air as possible, and transfer the whole shooting match in to a half gallon plastic container with lid and place in the coldest part of the deep freeze for at least 24 hours.

GINGER ICE CREAM

To make about half a gallon of ice cream

4 eggs
1 pt/600 ml double cream
4 oz/100 grms caster sugar
1 lb/450 grms jar of stem ginger
1 tablespoonful of syrup from the ginger jar
a glass of Stone's ginger wine

Method
We make this in precisely the same way as the **Coconut and Pistachio Ice Cream** except that instead of pistachio nuts, Malibu and coconut cream we fold in chopped ginger and some ginger syrup together with some ginger wine. A variation for even greater deliciousness is to add some roughly grated plain chocolate.

INDIVIDUAL AUTUMN PUDDINGS

As its name implies this is a sequel to Summer Pudding using fruits that are
available in Autumn.

To serve 6	**6 slices of medium sliced one day old bread**
	12 oz/325 grms blackberries
	3 eating apples
	6 oz/150 grms dried apricots
	4 oz/100 grms prunes
	2 large pears
	5 plums
	3 oz/75 grms sultanas
	4 - 6 oz/100 - 150 grms caster sugar
	1/2 pt/300 ml orange juice
	1 cinnamon stick
	1 teaspoonful of mixed spice
	half an orange
	half a lemon
	3/4 pt/450 ml clotted cream
Equipment	**6 x 3 in. diameter ramekins**

Preparation

It is important to make this dish early in the day if you are planning to
serve it in the evening.

Prepare the apples, apricots, prunes, pears and plums and roughly chop
them. Next take a heavy based saucepan and tip in the fruit together with
the blackberries, sultanas, caster sugar, orange juice, cinnamon, mixed spice
and the half orange and half lemon. Bring briefly to the boil and simmer
uncovered, stirring from time to time, for about 25 to 30 minutes. Taste
and adjust the sugar and lemon juice levels. Allow to cool and store in the
fridge.

Method

The assembly of these pudding should take place two to three hours before
they are due to be served to allow them to set properly. Start by taking six
ramekins. We need to line the walls of these with white bread and the best
way to do this is to use a medium sliced loaf. Taking one slice at a time,
trim off the crusts and you should find that the remaining bread is more
than enough to line the walls, if it is cut in half. It is essential that the two
halves fit snugly with no gaps.

Now reach for the stewed fruit that you have prepared earlier and which by now should be cold. Spoon in to the middle of each ramekin to a point where it is piled up so that when covered with greaseproof paper and heavy weights the mixture is compacted down. These should stand in the fridge until the moment when they are served.

Hopefully there will be some of the stewed fruit mixture left over. This should be pureed, sieved and poured in to a jug, adding orange juice if necessary to make the consistency of single cream.

To serve - Turn out each ramekin on to the middle of a plate using a table knife to release the bread from the walls of the ramekin. Finish by pouring over some of the fruit puree and serving with a dollop of clotted cream and a mint leaf for decoration.

WINTER PUDDING

Unlike **Summer** and **Autumn Pudding** this is not wrapped in sliced bread but otherwise it is a sequel.

To serve 4 to 6	1 1/2 lb/675 grms cooking apples
	6 oz/150 grms dried apricots
	6 oz/150 grms sultanas
	7 oz/175 grms demerara sugar
	6 oz/150 grms brown breadcrumbs
	4 oz/100 grms unsalted butter
	3/4 pt/450 ml thick double cream
	2 glasses of water
	the juice of a lemon
	1 teaspoonful of ground cinnamon
	a shot of brandy or calvados

Equipment	4 to 6 fluted glasses

Preparation

We start by preparing and chopping the apples and apricots. Cook them in the water with the sultanas, cinnamon, lemon juice, calvados and 4 oz/100 grms of the sugar in an uncovered pan for 10 to 20 minutes until soft. Allow to cool. In a heavy based frying pan melt the butter and cook the breadcrumbs shaking regularly until they are crisp. Only then stir in the remaining sugar and cook for a minute or two longer, stirring all the time.

Assembly

The idea is to layer the fruit and breadcrumbs in the fluted glasses rounding off with a generous layer of double cream. It is best to thoroughly chill the puddings before serving and at this last minute a little calvados in to the top of each pudding before the cream is poured on adds to the excitement. Serve with home-made biscuits or Cigarette Russes.

BREAD AND BUTTER PUDDING

To serve 4 to 6   8 - 10 medium slices of crustless white bread
1/2 pt/300 ml milk
1/2 pt/300 ml double cream
4 eggs
5 oz/125 grms caster sugar
4 oz/100 grms unsalted butter
6 oz/150 grms sultanas
1 tablespoonful of Marsala or sweet sherry
4 tablespoonfuls of water
1 teaspoonful of mixed spice
2 dessertspoonfuls of apricot jam
the grated rind of two oranges

Equipment   3 in. deep oval gratin or souffle dish

Preparation
Soak the sultanas in the Marsala or sherry and water. Preheat the oven to gas mark 4/350 degrees.

Method
Start by making the custard mixture. Pour the milk, double cream and orange rind in to a saucepan and heat gently to a point just short of boiling. In a separate bowl whisk the eggs and beat in the sugar. Now pour over the hot milk and cream, whisking all the time. Finish by stirring in the mixed spice.

Next take the dish and distribute half the sultanas across the bottom, followed by half the bread which should be buttered and cut to fit the shape of the dish. Pour over half the custard mixture and allow to stand for about 10 minutes before repeating the process again with the remaining sultanas, bread and egg custard. Allow to stand for another 10 minutes or so before placing in the middle of the oven and cooking for 35 minutes. At this stage brush the apricot jam over the top and return to the oven for another 10 minutes or so. Take care to see that the top does not get too brown - protect it with a sheet of greaseproof paper if necessary.

Before serving allow the pudding to cool somewhat as this is nicer served warm than hot. This can be accompanied by a raspberry or blackcurrant sauce.

HOLLANDAISE SAUCE

To make 1/2 pt/300 ml

8 oz/200 grms salted butter
the juice of two lemons
3 egg yolks
half a teaspoonful of Dijon mustard

Method
This is a simple method of making a light creamy hollandaise using lemon juice and mustard rather than the more traditional reduction of vinegar with a bay leaf.
Start by thoroughly melting the butter, taking care not to brown it at all. Next combine the egg yolks, lemon juice and mustard in the top half of a double saucepan away from the heat. Then place over the heat and whisk until thick and smooth (not scrambled!)
Transfer this in to an earthenware mixing bowl ready for the melted butter to be poured on in a thin stream, whisking all the time. The finished article should be smooth, creamy and shining with no sign of separation. There should be no need for further seasoning. Set aside keeping the sauce at kitchen temperature. Serve as soon as possible.

If the sauce should separate:- Do not be dismayed! Simply return the mixture to the heat in a double saucepan and bring up to a temperature hotter than blood heat but less than boiling. Take a clean bowl and fill it with boiling water - this warms the bowl. Pour off the hot water leaving a teaspoonful in the bottom. Now simply pour the separated hollandaise in a very fine stream on to the water whisking continuously. There are other methods of retrieving hollandaise but this way is fool proof.

To reheat leftover sauce:- Follow the instructions above.

BECHAMEL SAUCE

Ingredients for 2 pts/1.2 litres

2 pts/1.2 litres of milk
2 oz/50 grms plain flour
2 oz/50 grms butter
half an onion
1 bay leaf
2 cloves
salt and freshly ground black pepper

Method

Start by making an onion cloute - stud the peeled onion with the bay leaf and cloves. Bring this together with the milk to the boil in a heavy based uncovered saucepan. Simmer for 10 minutes and remove the cloute.

In a separate pan melt the butter before adding the flour to make a roux. Continue to cook for 2 minutes, stirring all the time. It is vital that a bechamel sauce should be absolutely smooth and the best way to achieve this is to pour the warm milk a little at a time on to the roux whisking vigorously until thick. Allow to simmer for no more than 5 minutes. Season to taste. Use as required.

BREAD SAUCE

1/2 pt/300 ml milk
2 0z/50 grms fresh white breadcrumbs
1 small onion
1 bay leaf
2 cloves
2 tablespoonfulls of white wine vinegar
a sprig of parsley
salt and freshly ground black pepper

Method

Firstly take the onion, peel it and make a cloute by pinning the bay leaf to it with the cloves. Next gently heat the milk with the onion cloute and continue cooking until the onion is soft. Top up the milk to the original level. Remove the onion and stir in the breadcrumbs, white wine vinegar and parsley. Simmer for at least 10 minutes, adjust the seasoning as necessary. Remember this sauce is delicious served cold with leftovers so make plenty!

ESPAGNOLE SAUCE

The backbone of any good commercial kitchen such as The Hungry Monk is always to have a quantity of first class stocks together with espagnole sauce in your fridge. There are a number of recipes in this book where we suggest you add espagnole sauce and we therefore give below a recipe that allows you to make 2 pints which can be frozen in ice trays to use in small quantities.

Ingredients for 2 pts/1.2 litres

>3 oz/75 grms good dripping
>1 carrot
>1 onion
>1 stick of celery
>some mushroom stalks
>1 rasher of streaky bacon
>3 oz/75 grms plain flour
>2 rounded tablespoonfuls of tomato puree
>1 tablespoonful of Worcestershire sauce
>1 bay leaf
>a bouquet garni
>2.5 pts/1.5 litres of meat or vegetable stock
>salt and freshly ground black pepper

Preparation

Peel and finely dice the onion and carrot. Finely slice the celery and bacon.

Method

Melt the dripping in a large saucepan and fry the onion, carrot, celery, mushroom stalks and bacon until golden brown. Then tip in the flour and continue to cook for 2 or 3 minutes, stirring briskly. Gradually pour in the stock, together with the rest of the ingredients. Bring to the boil and simmer for 10 minutes. Season. Reduce the sauce by simmering, uncovered for about 30 minutes. Strain in to a jug ready for use or cool and freeze in ice cube trays to be used as required.

Printed in Great Britain by St Edmundsbury Press Ltd, Bury St Edmunds, Suffolk.